Nietzsche and Wagner

Nietzsche and Wagner

A Lesson in Subjugation

Joachim Köhler
Translated by Ronald Taylor

Yale University Press
New Haven and London

For Carol

Set in Walbaum
Printed in Great Britain by St Edmundsbury Press

Library of Congress Catalog Card Number 98–87833
ISBN 0–300–07640–1
A catalogue record for this book is available from the British Library.

10 9 8 7 6 5 4 3 2 1

Permission to reproduce illustrations is kindly acknowledged:
Stiftung Weimarer Klassik 1, 3, 7, 10; Richard-Wagner-Museum, Bayreuth: 2, 5,
9; Rowohlt Verlag Archives, Reinbek bei Hamburg: 4, 6, 8, 11, 12, 13, 14

I should like to express my thanks to Thomas Karlauf of the Rowohlt Verlag
Berlin for suggesting a book on this subject and for his valuable cooperation in
its publication. (J.K.)

Contents

1
A Visit to the Underworld

It is easy to lose one's way in the myth of Dionysus and Ariadne. As tortuous and enigmatic as the labyrinth in which it starts and to which it returns, it moves in a circle; like the legendary labyrinth itself, it has neither beginning nor end. No one who ventures down its twisting paths can know what awaits him round the next bend – a beautiful princess, a savage warrior or, lurking at the heart of the maze itself, a man-eating monster. Or perhaps it will be an encounter with a devious deity by the name of Dionysus, who, from behind the masks of Ariadne, Theseus and Minotaur, plays spiteful tricks on anyone who enters his kingdom, a kingdom seen by some as symbolizing the perplexing paths of life, by others, the sullen despair of the underworld.

Indeed, even the poets of antiquity themselves did not know for certain what happened in the palace of Knossos to cause the proud princess Ariadne to help Theseus, a complete stranger, to murder her half-brother the Minotaur, a man with the head of a bull, and then escape from the maze by means of a ball of wool. After slaying the monster, Theseus took the traitor with him across the sea to the island of Naxos, where he intended to wed her. But all came to naught when the bridegroom disappeared, either because he had reached the end of his tether or had become homesick for Athens, or because Dionysus, the master of disguise, had concocted some story which made it seem advisable to beat a hasty retreat. The only thing known for certain is that Ariadne, spurned and wounded to the quick, was left weeping on the sandy shore of Naxos, praying for an end to her suffering and her guilt-ridden young life.

Her lamentation did not go unheard. The god Dionysus came, the lord both of life in full bloom and of Hades, travelling across the sea to release her from her agony. How he did this is a matter of dispute. Some maintain that, as punishment for her manifold acts of treachery towards not only her half-brother and the royal family but also towards the god himself, to whom she was pledged, Dionysus had Artemis slay her with an arrow. Others held to the view that the god restored the grieving woman's joy in life by his embrace, either there and then, on the beach where Theseus had deserted her, or behind the swirling mists on a lofty mountain, or in some garlanded paradise known only to the imagination.

Thus Dionysus and Ariadne came to be wed, their ecstatic union resolving the antitheses between the divine and the human, between male and female, between life and death. And as an act of cosmic magic to seal the act, the god, crazed with visions of love and death, hurled his bride's headdress into the night sky, where it should remain for all time as a sign that she had joined the ranks of the immortal.

Homer painted a different picture. He describes Odysseus discovering Ariadne at the entrance to Hades – still the 'beautiful Princess' but dead, like the other spirits: Artemis had consigned her to the underworld on Dionysus's orders. 'Pale with horror', Odysseus then flees from the ghostly labyrinth.

Friedrich Nietzsche, through whose life this myth runs in an unbroken thread, also wrote a poem called 'Klage der Ariadne' ('Ariadne's Lament'), in which he gives yet another version of the story. The final draft of this chilling threnody, which occupied him over many years, dates from the winter of 1888, when, in Turin, his madness broke out and he began to sign his letters 'Dionysus'. In the flush of exaltation that accompanied his mental breakdown, he felt sublime sensations of divinity and, like Dionysus, his role model, exchanged one persona for another at will. At one moment he saw himself as Shakespeare or Caesar, at the next as King of Italy or as Wagner, a mortal enemy he pursued with all the savagery he had at his command. And these figures all revealed themselves to him as incarnations of the one god, the god Dionysus, with whom he knew himself to be identical.

On New Year's Day 1889 he signed the dedication of his collection of poems *Dionysos-Dithyramben* (*Dithyrambs of Dionysus*) with the god's name, even giving him a role in the poem 'Ariadne's Lament'. Here, lying on the beach on the island of Naxos and yearning for her lover's ardent embrace, the forsaken Princess finds herself being tormented by a cruel god who hides behind the clouds. She is racked with strange fevers, jagged splinters of ice pierce her body as she moans that the mysterious god has consigned her to everlasting torment. As he gazes down mockingly on her with the lust of a voyeur, she twists and turns in her frantic efforts to escape his 'barb'. Odysseus might have seen her in a similar state of agony at the entrance to the underworld. Pale and trembling, she despairs of any alleviation of her suffering, for the god whose wrath she has aroused is Hades, the sinister side of Dionysus, god of Love. Nietzsche's Ariadne calls him 'god the hangman'.

Lying in his Turin garret, convinced that he was the god Dionysus, the demented Nietzsche gave himself away. His Ariadne was meant to cry: 'Strike me harder! Strike me again! Pierce and break this heart!' Instead, when he made his *Dithyrambs* public –

'an unreserved favour' to mankind, as he put it – he gave the poem an erotic twist and had her cry to Dionysus; 'Pierce me deeper! Pierce me with your dripping shaft!', begging him to penetrate her with his 'cruel barb' and bring her the consolation for which Nietzsche longs in one of his other poems to Dionysus. Not surprisingly, the editors of his works quietly concealed this delight in pain and the obscene identification of the tormenting barb with the god's phallus.*

Scarcely has Ariadne uttered her cry to the god, 'hidden behind the lightning', than he makes his appearance. In Nietzsche's words, 'Dionysus becomes visible in a flash of emerald beauty'. But does he mean the waves of the emerald ocean that brought Dionysus's craft to the shores of Naxos, or the first stirrings of the erotic urge which he refers to in *Ecce Homo* as 'an emerald bliss, a divine tenderness such as no poet before me had known?' Ariadne will not have to wait long for the answer – everything points to a happy ending.

But this union of opposites is not to be consummated on this New Year's Day in the little room above the Piazza Carlo Alberto in Turin, with its post office from which Nietzsche sent his 'delirious missives'. There is no 'piercing', no 'dripping shaft'. The god has other ideas in mind. As Nietzsche, the pastor's son, is compelled to utter his thoughts, so too is his master, the god. But the disjointed phrases that Dionysus speaks bring Ariadne to her senses - and with her the reader of these odes:

> Be wise, Ariadne!
> Thou hast little ears – thou hast my ears.
> Fill them with words of wisdom!

*Translator's note: The sexual overtones of this passage, both in the author's text and in Nietzsche's autograph, derive from the word-play between the German *triff* ('strike') and *trief* ('drip').

Must we not hate each other before loving each other?
I AM THY LABYRINTH

These are hardly the words of a lover, let alone of a love-sick god anxious to consummate the union there and then. He is behaving like a teacher, issuing warnings, while drawing attention in a singularly discourteous manner to a physiological peculiarity of the Princess' of which both Classical mythology and the reader are unaware. What comfort can she draw from having small ears, like him? And what of the final enigmatic line, in which, instead of carrying her off to sensual delights on the pinnacle of Olympus, he reveals himself as a subterranean labyrinth, as Hades, from which there is no escape? You will never find release from my grasp, he is saying − I shall hold you in my clutches till the end of time.

There was only one Ariadne who could have felt that Dionysus's words were addressed to her. In contrast to Nietzsche, she really did have large ears, and he had made fun of the fact in his *Götzen-dämmerung* (*Twilight of the Idols*). Here, in the role of divine arbiter of taste, the spiteful Dionysus seizes his bride, the Princess Ariadne, by the ears in a particularly flagrant example of human nastiness. 'Why, O why, divine Dionysus,' she cries, 'do you pull me by the ears?' To which he replies roughly: 'I find a sort of humour in your ears. Why are they not longer still?'

But the 'Princess' whom Nietzsche was trying to provoke did not answer, since she had not read *The Twilight of the Idols* and had in any case little desire to concern herself with its author. Whereupon, having long portrayed himself to those in the know as her 'philosophical lover', Neitzsche resolved to bring the matter to a climax.

At the beginning of January 1889 he took the liberty of sending a message to Cosima, widow of Richard Wagner. 'I am informed', he wrote, 'that a certain divine jester has recently finished his *Dithyrambs of Dionysus*.' The sentence was not as casual as it looked. For Nietzsche took it for granted that the Mistress of Bayreuth would recognize who was doing her the honour of addressing her — not the Friedrich Nietzsche, once the flag-bearer of the Wagnerian cause, who had now become its arch-enemy, but the god Dionysus himself, to whom his disciple had dedicated the poems, including 'Ariadne's Lament', in which Cosima played the part of the Princess.

Barely had he posted his letter than the 'divine jester' began to have second thoughts. Would Cosima understand why she, of all people, had been deemed worthy to receive this Dionysian message, with its reference to ears and labyrinths? Hurriedly he began to write a second letter which would make everything crystal clear: 'To Princess Ariadne, my beloved. . .' But were they *his* words, the words of a retired professor? No — the writer was the god who had been 'like Buddha to the Indians', at times also like Voltaire and Napoleon, even like Wagner, and who now returned in the form of 'the victorious Dionysus, who will turn the earth into a place of rejoicing'. Lest Cosima should feel excessively flattered, the industrious god added: 'Not that I have a great deal of time.'

Nor had he. Only a few days were left to Nietzsche in which to allow his megalomania free rein in his Turin garret, which he had decked out as a temple, staging Dionysian orgies for his own delight and improvising at the piano for hours on themes from Wagner. Now and again he would join the crowds in the street below, explaining to passers-by that he was a god who, in deference to the inferiority of humankind, had assumed the guise of a clown: they would be no more capable of enduring his real presence, he told them, than Semele had been able to bear the appearance of Zeus amid the thunder and lightning. Then he would climb back to his room at the top of the house and perform Dionysian dances in the nude, secretly watched by his landlady.

Forty-four years of age, stricken with syphilis, he received a visit on 8 January 1889 − not, as he had expected, from the King and Queen of Italy, but from his friend Franz Overbeck, professor of theology in Basel. In Overbeck's honour he performed a ritual dance − a spectacle that, wrote his scandalized friend, 'symbolized in the most gruesome manner the orgiastic frenzy that lies at the root of Greek tragedy'. Thereupon Overbeck took the mad Dionysus by train to Basle and put him in an asylum.

Viewed from a distance, Wahnfried, the bulky stone villa in Bayreuth where Wagner spent his final years, is uninviting. The early twentieth-century visitor, passing the bronze statue of Ludwig the Magnanimous and approaching the house, its two-storeyed central section rising windowless to the flat roof, felt reminded of a mausoleum set round with cypresses. Those permitted to enter the shrine and pay their homage − kings and emperors, even the Tsar of Bulgaria − found themselves in a lofty hall in which the light, shining down from above, fell on two marble busts − those of Richard and Cosima Wagner. As the sculptor's hand had turned the Master's gnome-like, yet dignified appearance into a polished, elegant expression of Apollonian serenity, so too Cosima's features, including a nose and mouth that Nietzsche's sister Elisabeth was not the only one to find 'too big', have been given a quality of classical timelessness. After the lord of Wahnfried died in Venice in 1883 and was buried in the garden behind the house, rule passed to the widow. There was an air of immortality about the place.

In the mezzanine above, where her children used to play, lay the diva in person. Since 1906, when she first fell prey to colic-like attacks, doctors had advised her to rest, and she left her room only to take a walk or to make one of her regular trips to an Italian spa. Nietzsche, whose Dionysian missives she had found highly obnoxious, was long since dead. She had assumed complete control of her husband's legacy, including the Bayreuth Festival and her numerous family. Below her was the room in which Wagner had assembled everything of consequence from his three-score-years-and-ten – assembled there once and for all. Nothing had been moved since his death. Wahnfried was not a museum but a shrine. If one had to speak, then it had to be in hushed tones.

But the most sacred of the relics stood in Cosima's room – the red sofa from the Palazzo Vendramin where Wagner had breathed his last. Here too lay the watch that she had given him and that had slipped out of his pocket while he was in the throes of death. His last words had been, not 'My Cosima!', but 'My watch!' Now it was ticking again. Portraits looked down on her from the walls – her father Franz Liszt and her mother Marie d'Agoult, her sister Blandine and her brother Daniel, King Ludwig of Bavaria, who had helped to finance Wahnfried – all dead. And everywhere the Master himself – a likeness by Lenbach, a bust on the mantelpiece. At night time she spoke to them. From the window she could see the grave that had been prepared for her. Indeed, she was actually breaking an arrangement by still being alive, for, as Wagner had confided to the King, they had agreed that she would follow him into the grave a week later. But it was to be another forty-seven years before her ashes were laid to rest beneath the granite slab in the garden, by the side of their dogs and parrots.

Cosima knew she had become a living cult object, and that was as she wished it to be. Only the select few were admitted into her regal presence. Draped in flowing robes, she would recline on her *chaise-longue*, her white hair gathered in a classical knot, as Wagner had preferred it, and receive her humble subjects, who, as her granddaughter Friedelind put it, 'stood there as if in front of an altar'. After they had left, Dora, her maid, poured her a glass of beer, while a parrot imitated the gurgling sound with uncanny accuracy. The parrot also had in its repertoire an imitation of

Cosima's daughter Eva burping, and whenever the unfortunate woman came up the stairs to bring her mother her meal or to take down a letter, the bird would put on its spiteful performance. More often, however, it gurgled, for, according to Winifred Wagner, Cosima's daughter-in-law, the old lady was 'very partial' to a drink.

In the years leading up to her death in 1930, Cosima retreated more and more into the past, directing rehearsals with casts of singers long since gone and lying for hours in a state of trance, as the family described it. Here she made contact with the dead. She was seized with convulsions, her body was racked with pain and her eyesight began to fail. 'It is like being cut off from the world,' she lamented to her daughters. In September 1923, as she lay half-dead, half-alive, a young man with emaciated features and wearing lederhosen visited Wahnfried. Like Cosima Adolf Hitler saw himself as Wagner's spokesman on earth. Before paying his respects in the temple of the Holy Grail, emblem of his own deranged philosophy, he had visited the racialist philosopher Houston Stewart Chamberlain, Eva's bed-ridden husband, and received his blessing. Bowing in reverence, he now entered the Wagner villa and tiptoed his way round the hall, passing from one memento to another 'as though he were looking at the relics in a cathedral'. One wonders whether he was admitted to the *grande dame's* chamber and pressed her wizened hand. At all events her granddaughter heard him announced as 'the saviour of Germany', and it is equally certain that Eva read to her mother from *Mein Kampf*, proofs of which were sent direct to Wahnfried from the publisher.

Whether the book made any impression on Cosima, we cannot tell. In her 'last words', preserved by her daughters like the utterances of an oracle, Voltaire and Eva's canary are mentioned, and the name of Houston Stewart Chamberlain occurs frequently – that of Wagner himself less so. Hitler makes no appearance. Nor does Nietzsche. Maybe, as Cosima once said, he had 'sunk into oblivion, which is sometimes a good thing'.

His mind deranged, Nietzsche had already reached his journey's end by the summer of 1897. Having spent periods in asylums in Basel and Jena, as well as in his mother's house in Naumburg, he now found fame awaiting him, the fame of the heroic herald of the Superman, enthroned in the villa belonging to his sister, Elisabeth Förster-Nietzsche. The red-brick villa with its slate roof stood on a bare hill overlooking Weimar. In the winter it was exposed to the wind, in the summer it was at the mercy of the sun, which led the local inhabitants to dub it Sunstroke House. A windmill nearby had had its sails ripped off in a gale — 'a metaphor for our existence,' Elisabeth observed. Not that she had anything to complain of. For her brother, who, while still capable of coherent speech, had called himself 'a poor Lazarus', had turned himself into a national cult figure. She published his works, which became bestsellers, and as his message captured the world, so she became his prophet.

Nietzsche's success arrived only with his madness. In Turin, shortly before the end came, he was an almost completely unknown down-at-heel writer who took irregular meals and counted every penny. The various places in Italy where he found accommodation — 'hide-outs' he called them — had been unheated, even in winter, and since his mother was saving for his future, he was given only a second-class room in the asylum. Thanks to the machinations of his sister, the fame of his works, enhanced by the aura that surrounded his insanity, led to a new-found prosperity for her.

The decisive change in his fortunes was already apparent when he arrived in Weimar in the April of 1897. His sister, small of stature, attended by servants in livery, accompanied him in a specially reserved Pullman car on the train from Naumburg to Weimar, where they were permitted to use the station entrance reserved for the Grand Duke and his family. With the curtains

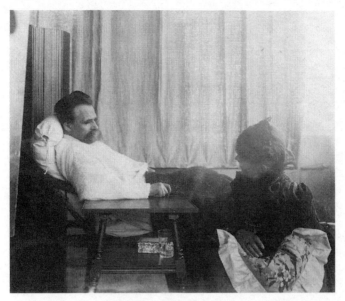

1 Friedrich Nietzsche on his sick-bed with his sister, 1899, the year
before his death.

drawn in his private carriage, he reached his destination in the
middle of the night.

As the story has it, when the coach drew up in front of the
villa, Nietzsche burst out, 'Palazzo! Palazzo!' Accustomed to simple
cottages, garrets and asylum cells, he must have found the spacious
salon with its crimson plush furniture like the entrance to a new,
higher reality – perhaps even like a return to Wagner's world of
silks and satins. And had not Wagner died in an Italian palazzo? As
though he himself were no longer in the land of the living, his
own portrait looked down on him from all the walls; sumptuously
bound copies of his works were arranged in glass-fronted
bookcases, and in the middle of the room stood his old upright
piano. In the early days of his illness he had often improvised on
it for hours; now it was an item in an exhibition, destined for the
celebration of his own compositions.

In his deranged state, music was the only medium that could
still get through to him. In his mother's house he had been

2 The ailing Cosima Wagner with her family, 1917.

fascinated by a mechanical music-box that played the Bridal Chorus from Wagner's *Lohengrin* – at Christmas 1893 it had seemed to him 'the most attractive item in the whole house'. In Weimar, too, music was now one of the few rays of light to penetrate the gloom of his existence. 'If someone suggested making music,' noted a visitor, 'he became agitated and uttered a series of ugly, incoherent sounds, a horrible moaning noise'. But once the music began, 'his features became transformed into an expression of indescribable ecstasy.' And if the name of Wagner happened to be mentioned, 'he never failed to say: "I loved that man dearly."'

While his sister received the intellectual elite of Europe in the salon, basking in his reflected glory, Nietzsche eked out a miserable existence on his bed in the room above, a live exhibit in his own personal museum. Like an audience with Cosima in Bayreuth, admittance to his room represented the climax of every pilgrim's visit, an awestruck visit to the Superman with his bushy moustache, enveloped in the prophet's mantle, his brown eyes now staring, now suddenly squinting or rolling from side to side, now hiding behind his thick eyebrows. He no longer spoke, no longer showed any reaction. His hands, their veins a greenish-purple, lay on the bed rug like a plaster cast. The only movement was from his eyes, which rolled from one side to the other before vanishing into oblivion.

In 1931, three decades after Nietzsche's death, Hitler paid a visit to the Weimar villa. Standing in reverence before the marble bust, he mused on *The Will to Power*. The now aged Elisabeth, who had become so shrivelled that one visitor to the house called her a 'pygmy queen', presented Hitler with two sacred souvenirs. One was a work entitled *General Petition against the Rampant Power of the Jews*, which her late husband, Bernhard Förster, had delivered to Bismarck in 1880; the other was her brother's sword, which looked like a harmless walking-stick. As late as 1943, in the middle of the Second World War, Hitler still saw a connection between the destruction of the Jews and the challenge of Nietzsche's Superman to live a more intense life, a life of heightened awareness. 'That is why', said Hitler, Zarathustra's terrible disciple, as Goebbels recorded in his diaries, 'Nietzsche is inevitably far closer to the way we see the world than is Schopenhauer, for the task of philosophy is to simplify and to intensify life, not to cover it with a veil of pessimism.'

The nationalistic gatherings held in his honour in the salon below passed the suffering Nietzsche by. Only after dark, when the visitors had left and recorded their experiences in their diaries, were sounds heard coming from his cell. The inhabitants of the house were frightened by a great roaring and shouting, audible even in the street below. 'Two or three long, savage, moaning cries came from his room,' wrote one guest in October 1897, 'which he delivered with all the power at his command, then all went quiet.' Another wrote of 'savage roars of despair that rent the night air, sounding as though they came from a mortally wounded beast'.

The sufferings of the 'living corpse' came to an end in August 1900. Elisabeth was his sole heir. Nietzsche had hoped to be buried by a mountain lake in Switzerland but Elisabeth had his remains laid to rest beside his father, the Protestant pastor, in a little village near Naumburg, where his tragic life had begun fifty-six years earlier.

2

Learning the Art of Self-Sacrifice

'The first event that impressed itself on my dawning consciousness', wrote Nietzsche, 'was my father's illness.' The year was 1848 and he was four at the time. For eleven months the young Friedrich watched his father endure agonies which, as his mother put it, 'pierced her to the quick' – agonies of paralysis, of convulsions, of failing eyesight and finally of dementia. Carl Ludwig Nietzsche had been a country parson renowned for his extravagant piety. Now his cries of torment could be heard in the street outside his house until, the following year, he died. His mysterious disease was described as 'softening of the brain'. His son's dreams were to be plagued by these visions for decades to come.

He even dreamt of his father's return. Six months after Carl Ludwig's death Friedrich had a vision in which the grave opened and a white, shrouded figure emerged to carry 'little Joseph', Friedrich's younger brother, back down with him into the depths. The dream came true, and after Joseph's death the rest of the family – the widowed Franziska and the two children Friedrich and Elisabeth – moved to the town of Naumburg, where they occupied a couple of gloomy back rooms as boarders in their grandmother's house. They were sustained by the memory of their departed father, who became the inspiration for young Fritz's education. The local citizens admiringly called him 'the little pastor', but they could have had no inkling of how he was haunted by the wails of his dying father.

Cherishing a longing for the divine and at the same time obsessed by the fear of hell, Nietzsche developed into the perfect pupil. Under the pressure of his mother's ambitions he began to write poetry and compose music, leaving his contemporaries far behind as far as knowledge and eloquence were concerned. The price he paid for this was a lifetime of nightmares and migraines. 'Because he was a prodigy at Schulpforta [the famous boarding school to which his mother sent him],' wrote the historian Jacob Burckhardt, later a colleague at the University of Basel, 'people expected more and more prodigious achievements from him, so overtaxing his strength that his health became permanently damaged.'

His élite school introduced him not only to a strict code of discipline but also to a new ideal. The saviour on the cross gave way to images of the gods of Greece. In the company of his friends he dreamt of the return of classical Athens, of the heroic deeds of Castor and Pollux, of the cultivation of philosophical wisdom in Plato's Symposium. In Naumburg he had recited prayers with a fervour that had brought tears to his listeners' eyes; now he composed love poems to his friends in classical metres.

He himself also became the object of such poems. Over a period of years Ernst Ortlepp, translator of Shakespeare and Byron, wrote lines in Nietzsche's poetry album that express a tender but unmistakable passion for his young friend. 'Never did I think', wrote Ortlepp, 'that I would ever love again.' For Nietzsche, the sixty-year-old Ortlepp, who dressed in the robes of a priest and loved to declaim in the tones of a preacher, became a substitute father figure. In fact, Ortlepp was the very opposite of a village pastor. He sang blasphemous songs, recited from the 'sinner' Byron and was often to be found wandering the countryside in a drunken state, which eventually led to his being jailed as a public nuisance.

In the taverns around Schulpforta, however, Ortlepp's eccentric genius delighted the spellbound students with piano improvisations and shocked them with what were called his 'demonic ballads'. This too reminded Nietzsche of his father, who used to improvise for hours at the piano and sing Schumann *lieder*. 'When I was young,' Nietzsche later recalled, 'I made contact with a dangerous deity, and I would not like to repeat what things scarred my consciousness – good things as well as bad.' It was in this figure of Ortlepp, the bibulous poet, that Nietzsche first encountered the two-faced Dionysus, god of sensuous pleasure but also of the fear of death. In 1864, the year Nietzsche graduated from Schulpforta, Ortlepp fell into a ditch in a drunken stupor and broke his neck. Nietzsche described him as 'a friend who sent bolts of lightning into the dark recesses of my youth'. But for as long as he lived he did not breathe a word about the nature of their relationship.

It is very likely that Ortlepp, whose *Polish Lyrics* Nietzsche mentions in 1888 in his *Ecce Homo*, also told Nietzsche about Wagner. Ortlepp and Wagner had met in Leipzig at the beginning of the 1830s and, together with Heinrich Laube of the revolutionary Young German movement, had discussed such subjects as the emancipation of the flesh and the rebirth of antiquity. Wagner, inspired, like Ortlepp, by the Poles' struggle for freedom, composed an overture at this time called *Polonia*, and Ortlepp was one of the first to foretell a great future for him. 'We are convinced', he wrote in a review, 'that Wagner will achieve great things.' Caught up in the revolutionary spirit that finally issued in the events of 1848, the twenty-year-old student Wagner and his poet friend felt that the ultimate liberation of mankind was within their grasp. Until that moment came, they continued to sit in their favourite Leipzig café, enjoying ice cream and Turkish coffee.

The same café became Nietzsche's favourite haunt when he arrived in Leipzig in 1864 to read Classics. Here he would join his friend Erwin Rohde to talk excitedly about the riding lessons they were taking together and to share his enthusiasm for their philosophical demi-god Schopenhauer. And here, one winter afternoon four years later, he was to spend a restless three quarters of an hour drinking cocoa and reading the satirical journal *Kladderadatsch*, before his first meeting that evening with Wagner, who was staying in his native city at the time in conditions of extreme secrecy.

From Ortlepp's time in Schulpforta onwards, the name of Wagner constantly recurs in Nietzsche's notes. His poems are spiced with quotations from *Tristan,* and the Nordic sources on which Wagner drew for his *Ring des Nibelungen* inspired Nietzsche to write an opera on the gruesome Ermanrich legend. But for Wagner's music, by contrast, he had no sympathy. In a list of his favourite composers dating from the spring of 1868 we find the names of Beethoven, who induced in him feelings of 'sublime exuberance' and the exciting sensation of being 'intoxicated with champagne', and Schumann, who filled him with a 'pervasive serenity' and a 'warm self-pity', and whose *Scenes from Goethe's Faust* stood supreme in its 'glittering ecstasy'. But there was no place at that moment for Wagner's heroes – they were not refined enough for him.

A few months later everything changed. Friedrich Ritschl, his tutor at the university, introduced him to a number of committed Wagnerians, including Wagner's old comrade-in-arms Heinrich Laube, and Ritschl's wife offered him the prospect of meeting Wagner's sister Ottilie, who was married to the Leipzig professor Hermann Brockhaus. From having scorned Wagner's music he was now filled with enthusiasm for it. Summoning his friends, chief among them Erwin Rohde, he waxed lyrical about this 'philosophy

3 Nietzsche in his last year at school, 1864.

in sound' and held forth to the astonished Frau Ritschl on the virtues of Wagner's latest work, *Die Meistersinger von Nürnberg*. 'Every nerve in my body is tingling,' he wrote. 'Not for years have I experienced such abiding rapture.' Previously he had been repelled by this bombastic music. Now he discovered in the *Ring's* hero, Siegfried, the reincarnation of Apollo, and in the morbid

harmonies of *Tristan* the dark side of his own childhood, which
the pessimism of Schopenhauer had shown to represent a glimpse
into the tragic depths of life. 'What I find congenial about Wagner
is what I find congenial about Schopenhauer,' he confided to
Rohde, 'the ethical essence, the Faustian atmosphere, the Cross,
death and the grave.'

He even began to find interest in Wagner's stilted and
generally ridiculed revolutionary writings. Here was a different
Greece from that taught at the university. Here he discovered an
ideal vision of mankind which he was soon to make his own, a
vision of antiquity as a paradigm for the present, with the Greek
hero as god-like Superman and the tragedies of Aeschylus as the
forebears of Wagner's music dramas. He even proclaimed Wagner
a new 'Saint of the Arts', a prophet of the real antiquity who
relegated university professors to the rank of 'academic labourers'.
Yet 'every dim-wit historian of literature', Nietzsche concluded,
'considers he has the right to urinate on Wagner. Such has been his
martyrdom.'

On the evening of 8 November 1868, the twenty-four-year-old
student of Classics met the fifty-five-year-old martyr. By chance he
had seen him in the street the previous day, 'wearing an enormous
hat on his big head', and had been told in confidence that a letter
had just arrived from the young King of Bavaria addressed to 'the
great German composer Richard Wagner'. Now the young student
found himself standing in person in front of the stocky, mercurial
little composer 'in Hermann Brockhaus's very comfortable salon',
and, apart from the presence of 'a few old women', as he described
his hostess and Frau Ritschl, the evening became a tête-à-tête
between the two men. Wagner conversed wittily in his Saxon
dialect, amused the company by parodying characters from his
Meistersinger, now in his natural pitch, now in falsetto, and recited
excerpts from his autobiography. Finally, warmly assuring
Nietzsche, who hung on his every word, of his absolute devotion to

Schopenhauer, he shook the young man's hand cordially and invited him to his country house, Tribschen, on the shores of Lake Lucerne, 'to talk music and philosophy together'.

The auspices for their relationship were far less favourable on that evening than Nietzsche's animated account implied. Wagner's clowning in front of his family and Nietzsche was aimed at distracting attention from the uncomfortable public revelation of the adulterous affair he had been carrying on for years with Cosima, wife of his friend Hans von Bülow. Cosima was desperately trying to persuade her husband to divorce her, while the young King Ludwig, who had long suspected what was going on, had resolved to break with Wagner, the man he had idolized. Indeed, the letter he had just sent to 'the great German composer' contained a refusal to grant him an audience; moreover, the letter had been drafted not by the King himself but by his private secretary.

To this humiliation were added Wagner's worries about Cosima, who was three months pregnant. After a series of violent arguments she had refused to leave Munich with her four daughters, the city he regarded as 'enemy territory'. 'Cosima beside herself. Deep depression,' he wrote in his *Annals*. The only record of his meeting with the young university student from Leipzig is an entry that says simply, 'Dr Nietzsche' – a designation which anticipated Nietzsche's doctorate by five months.

Born in 1837, the illegitimate progeny of a liaison whose breakdown had been a traumatic experience for her, Francesca Gaetana Cosima Liszt spent her childhood not in the shadow of Hades, like Nietzsche, but in fear of desertion. Raised by an Austrian grandmother and a succession of governesses, she suffered, as she wrote, 'from having neither father nor mother'. A victim of circumstances, like Nietzsche, she internalized her given role to such an extent that even as a child she identified herself with Elisabeth in Wagner's *Tannhäuser*, the character whose destiny was to sacrifice herself for another, whose only thought was release from the bonds of the flesh, and who cherished but one desire — to become a saint or a martyr. Such was the role model Cosima had chosen for herself.

Her father, Franz Liszt, who disappeared from her life as though he had died, was the most famous pianist in Europe. He was also a notorious lady-killer who would have preferred to forget the three children who only served to remind him of his former mistress. But for their part the children — the vivacious Blandine, the 'less attractive and less refined Cosima', as her mother described her, and the sickly, withdrawn Daniel — made him into an idol at whose shrine they worshipped and for whose eventual return they longed in vain. Letters passed to and fro between them, the children's tender and affectionate, their father's stern and severe, sent to Paris from all corners of the continent. But he never returned himself. Instead Anna Liszt, the children's grandmother, turned their little apartment into a votive temple dedicated to her son. The walls were covered with portraits, laurel wreaths and decorations, while mounted on plinths stood marble busts, as though in honour of the dead. Indeed, had it not been for his occasional letters, the children would have believed that he really was no longer alive.

Marie d'Agoult, their mother, scion of an aristocratic line not without its blemishes, had fallen passionately in love with Liszt, nonchalantly turning her back on her status-conscious family. But after the breakdown of their domestic life together, with Liszt leaving to resume his career as an itinerant virtuoso, she too deserted her three young children and sought comfort in the bosom of her family. From that moment on, their father, himself little more than a memory, decreed that a basic principle of their upbringing should be that all mention of their mother's name be forbidden. The memory of Countess Marie d'Agoult was simply to be wiped out.

But she too abandoned her children. She could not take them to her mother, the high-principled daughter of a Frankfurt banker, because as far as the Countess de Flavigny was concerned, her grandchildren did not exist. Liszt, for his part, was far too occupied with concert tours and love-affairs to have any time for his family in their little Paris apartment. He had started a relationship with an intellectual married woman, Princess Carolyne von Sayn-Wittgenstein, whom he had met in Russia in 1847 and whose attentions he was unable to throw off for the rest of his life. A fanatical Catholic, she might have been expected to show a measure of Christian charity towards his children. But she was as heartless as their mother and completely taken up with the interests of her own daughter, Marie.

Liszt devoted himself to the ten-year-old Marie Wittgenstein – 'Magnolette', as she was called – in place of his own children, professing in a kind of love-letter that she was 'charm, kindness and wisdom itself, perfection in person. How blessed am I to experience the boundless rapture that you arouse in me!' When the Princess decided that his own children should be brought up under a strict regime, he raised no objection, and her governess, an old woman of seventy-two, was despatched to Paris by train to take the three virtual orphans under her oppressive, disciplinarian, unloving control. This was nothing new for Cosima, who, as she said, 'had from the beginning always been forced to obey'. At the same time her relationship with her father deteriorated. In her eyes, he had always been tied to the Princess's apron-strings. As a result of their relationship to their stepmother, she later wrote, 'we children, who worshipped him, were always brusquely rejected by him'. Nietzsche's recurrent nightmare centred on his father in death: Cosima's was dominated by the overwhelming figure of her stepmother in life.

As Cosima reached the age of puberty, her parents re-emerged, first her mother, who surreptitiously invited the children to snatch a glimpse of the luxury in which she was now living. She had become a writer, taking the masculine name — like a blond George Sand - of Daniel Stern, filling her mind with the history of the French Revolution, revelling in her now notorious affair with Liszt, smoking cigarillos and holding court in the magnificent salon of her 'Maison Rouge' before the fashionable authors and artists of the day. On one occasion Wagner had been among them and had held forth on his favourite subject — the liberation of mankind.

For the neglected children such visits were fleeting moments of excitement that ended with the return to their governess's prison. Sometimes their mother took them to the Louvre or the Comédie française, or had them play from Wagner's latest works. For Cosima these brief afternoon outings seemed like visits to 'the realm of bliss'.

There was happy news too from their father. After an absence of eight years he announced his intention of rejoining them and arrived in October 1853. But he was not alone. Their stepmother swept into the room, at her side her pretty and fashionably dressed young daughter — sixteen years old, the same as Cosima — who allowed herself to be courted by Liszt's friend Wagner. He was to recite excerpts from his new drama *Der junge Siegfried* in her honour.

The precocious young 'Magnolette' put the shy, drab Blandine and Cosima totally in the shade, and when their father set out on one of his popular coach rides amongst the chic society of the day, it was Marie he took with him, not his own daughters. 'It came as no surprise,' wrote Cosima later: 'all my childhood I was made to stay at home.' Nor did it surprise Marie. She remembered Cosima as 'somewhat awkward, with the eyes of a frightened deer in a hostile environment, a typically immature young creature, tall, bony, with a sallow complexion, a big mouth and a long nose'. When, after one of Wagner's dreaded lengthy readings from his own works, Marie ventured to crown him with a laurel wreath, she observed the 'blissful expression' on Cosima's face and 'the tears that poured down her angular nose'. Sensing a potential rival, she added spitefully: 'Wagner did not give the ugly creature a second glance.'

But the inhibited Cosima could also burst into sudden fits of rage which alternated with 'displays of affection pathological in their intensity', as Wagner later witnessed to his amazement. She compensated for the lack of physical attractiveness that led her to be dubbed 'stork' by skilfully projecting her qualities to the best advantage and by adopting a precocious emotionalism reminiscent of the Comédie française. This led Blandine to mock her as 'theatrical', while Marie accused her of 'offending people by her excessive self-centredness and her innate severity', which led men to brand her as 'unfeminine'. Such are the weapons of the born underdog.

But no sooner did Liszt appear than he vanished again. Not, however, that he left the children exposed to their mother's 'bad influence'. Instead he resorted to a stratagem designed to end their contact with her. Apparently as a treat, he invited them to his villa in Weimar, where he lived on a grand scale with the sanctimonious Princess Carolyne and the flirtatious Marie. Hardly had the children's initial joy at their reunion passed when the invitation turned out to be a trick. For instead of sending them back home to rejoin their beloved brother Daniel, Liszt despatched them to a new governess in Berlin, Franziska von Bülow, where there was no prospect of escape. Like a calculating politician, the Princess was using the girls as pawns in the struggle against her arch-enemy, Marie d'Agoult. Once again Cosima found herself betrayed and condemned to life imprisonment.

Since her divorce from Baron von Bülow the irritable Franziska had ruled the house in Berlin. Obsessed with her son Hans, who had in his turn replaced his father with the figures of Liszt and Wagner, Franziska assumed the role of the girls' chaperon, while

Hans became their piano teacher. Sooner or later, it was assumed, one or other of the girls would become his mistress, perhaps even his wife. In spite of his apparent opposition to the idea, it in fact suited Liszt admirably. If one of his daughters did marry the young Hans von Bülow, he reasoned, her illegitimacy would cease to be an issue, she would be removed from her mother's sphere of influence and her submission to his and the domineering Carolyne's authority guaranteed once and for all. Moreover, he had long regarded Bülow as his musical heir, whichever daughter he eventually married.

Six weeks after the two girls had been sent to the Bülow residence, Hans made his choice. In October 1855 Liszt gave his consent to the betrothal of his innocent seventeen-year-old Cosima to his favourite pupil. As it happened, on the same evening Bülow had just conducted the overture to *Tannhäuser*, the opera by his 'friend and father' Richard Wagner, and been booed. While the ladies returned disconsolately to their house in the Wilhelm-strasse, Liszt took the unhappy Hans on a tour of the Berlin night-spots before delivering him back home. 'At two o'clock in the morning,' he commented slily, 'I pushed Hans through the front door. A light was still burning but I did not go up.'

The light came from Cosima's room. Unwilling to go to bed, her mind pulsating with thoughts of Hans's self-sacrifice in the cause of Wagner's music, she wanted to make her own act of sacrifice and wait for his return, as Wagner's Elisabeth had waited for the guilty Tannhäuser. All the actors in the drama had summed up the situation, and the next morning the mismatch was settled. As Cosima, accustomed to blindly carrying out her father's wishes, surrendered herself to his admirer, and thus to her father himself, so Bülow, in embracing her, embraced his idol. 'The thought of moving closer to you, the person who above all others has given birth to and sustained my life hitherto and will continue to do so in the future, brings the consummation of all the happiness I can conceive on earth,' he effused, as though he were wooing the father, not the daughter. Cosima, he went on, not only bore his name but reflected his character. And Cosima, for her part, saw nothing unusual in this erotic charade because she had been brought up to idolize her father. The night of love that must have followed the disaster of the *Tannhäuser* overture was a ceremony performed by Hans and Cosima on the altar of their god, Franz Liszt.

It was no accident that it should have been Wagner's romantic opera of homage to Venus and divine forgiveness that led Cosima to surrender herself. She had known her father's piano transcription of the work for a long time and played parts of it to her mother in the 'Maison Rouge'. The transition from the impassioned, ecstatic Venusberg music to the reverential chorus of the pilgrims was the perfect symbol of her relationship to music. As the sound of a piano in her childhood used to make her pine for her distant parents, so now such sounds plunged her into a trance-like state of sublimated desire and a passionate craving for redemption.

'There is something frightening about the power of art,' she wrote, 'for it releases the demonic in us.' The words might have come from Nietzsche, for whom music was an expression of the Dionysian, transcending all boundaries, blurring the distinctions between the sexes and plunging the listener into a vortex of divine ecstasy. In the wake of such an experience, as Cosima also knew, everyday life suddenly became unbearable, the 'absurdities of our human existence exposed in a dazzling ray of light'. For Nietzsche, Wagner long remained the drug that caused intoxication. 'This, and nothing else,' he wrote later, 'is what I mean by the word Music when I talk of the Dionysian.' Cosima too would on occasion fall into a trance and, like him, see ghosts. Her family described her as having somnambulist tendencies, and Wagner, who had been attracted to mystery stories since boyhood, particularly since hearing Weber's *Der Freischütz*, was deeply impressed by the Delphic thoughts she uttered in her coma-like state.

Two years after the night when Liszt had pushed Hans von Bülow back into his house to join the waiting Cosima, their wedding took place. Her mother was not invited. Her grand-mother declined to attend, indicating from Paris that she found it a far from satisfactory match. That was a considerable under-statement. 'I wept the whole night before the wedding,' wrote Cosima. And although she dutifully insisted how much she loved her Hans, there was no disguising what she felt in the depths of her heart: 'I had the feeling I was making a great sacrifice.'

Since the newly-wed husband felt the urge to spend his honeymoon with someone he really loved, he travelled to see Wagner in Zurich, and Cosima was allowed to accompany him. For three weeks she saw for herself how much Wagner's new *Siegfried* meant to her husband — he described it as being 'like an act of deliverance from the sordidness of the world'. Wagner himself seemed caught up in this sordidness at the time, for he was carrying on an affair with Mathilde Wesendonk, wife of his host and patron, under her husband's very eyes, while his own dull, virtuous wife Minna, seized with jealousy, was made to serve them cold refreshments. When he crept back to Minna in the darkness, Mathilde had fits of jealousy in her turn. He then took out his irritation on the timid Cosima, teasing her in ways that increased her unease.

Bülow, meanwhile, had eyes only for the Master. 'I can conceive of nothing that could offer me such delight, such solace,' he wrote during his honeymoon — not, as one might expect, as the love of his new, young wife but 'as the company of this wonderful man whom one must revere as a God.' Immediately on his return to Berlin, he read the libretto of *Tristan und Isolde* and wrote to Wagner that he was celebrating 'something quite different from the usual kind of honeymoon, and my wife is in no way jealous'.

4 Cosima Wagner and her father, Franz Liszt — photo of 1867.

But here Bülow's ecstatic state was deceiving him, as Wagner could not fail to notice, confiding to his inamorata Mathilde Maier that 'from his earliest youth Bülow had shown a warmth and tenderness towards me that even made his wife jealous.'

Hans von Bülow had long been lost in the Wagnerian labyrinth, and instead of allowing his young wife to show him the way out of it, he drew her with him into the seductive web in which the Master had ensnared him. Wagner was looking for victims, and none better could be found than this young couple. Hans was completely in his clutches, while Cosima, repeatedly haunted since her wedding by thoughts of suicide, was only waiting for an opportunity to put an end to her life as Bülow's consort, by whatever means. After an ill-starred attempt to escape from her new prison, she begged a young friend of Wagner's called Karl Ritter, an unlikely *amoroso*, to kill her: otherwise she would drown herself in the waters of Lake Geneva. Wagner later wrote that she had always longed for death, 'had always stood on the brink of the abyss, prepared to throw herself off at any moment.'

But instead Cosima threw herself into the arms of the man who, like his Tannhäuser, had dallied among the pleasures of the Venusberg and never found the Elisabeth who would deliver him. Her husband, caught up in the excesses of his Wagner worship, only encouraged her. When, like Mary Magdalene, she fell on her knees before the Master, kissing his hands and bathing them in tears, Bülow did the same. He later wrote to the object of their adoration: 'She is always afraid that you will consider her childish and too insignificant to be able to love and understand you. Yet in truth she is one of the very few who are capable of just that.'

Such creatures are the stuff of sacrifice – with the difference that in this case the victim surrendered herself voluntarily, discovering ever new ways of capturing the mind of the lord of the labyrinth. 'After Wagner had played or recited something he had just written,' wrote Peter Cornelius, one of the Master's young friends and disciples, 'she would sink into a trance, like a sleep-walker, whispering gnomic prophesies. Wagner was profoundly impressed.'

Bülow had no objection to all this. As Cosima was at the root of his attachment to Liszt, so it was Cosima who now sealed his union with Wagner. Not long before she became pregnant with Wagner's first child, Bülow assured his sister that in his eyes his marriage was 'emphatically if surprisingly a happy one'. At the same time, being, as he put it, 'a person with feminine tendencies', he found his wife to be a woman 'not needful of my protection but rather in a position to offer me hers'. Soon it was no longer he who led the cult of the Master but she, the woman who would fall into a swoon over *Tristan*, would weep over *Lohengrin*, and then, the very next morning, would display the instincts of the confident business-woman in dealing with the marketing of Wagner's music. Husband and wife, observed Cornelius in Munich, where in 1864 the triangular relationship was to reach a dramatic climax, 'had completely identified with Wagner'.

It was only a question of time before Cosima and Wagner became one soul and one body. He gave her what Bülow − stiff and formal, a man, according to Cosima, who had no idea 'what pleased or pained a woman' − had failed to give her. Seen through her eyes, her adultery was inevitable, as she later insisted. With Bülow acting as intermediary, one idealized father figure had taken the place of another − where Liszt had once been, only Wagner would now be.

Although he later persistently denied it, Wagner's affair with Cosima was for him only one of many. She was not the first woman to lose her way in the Wagnerian maze. In November 1863, as he later dictated his life story to her, while she wrote down his words with a gold pen, they had resolved, 'sobbing and weeping, to pledge themselves each to the other'. But at that time various other women were still wandering through remote corners of his labyrinth − the aristocratic ladies Henriette von Bissing and Marie von Buch, nicknamed 'Mimi'; his Viennese mistress, the dancer Marie; the ever-present Mathilde Wesendonk, muse of *Tristan*; Mathilde Maier and the overwrought actress Friederike Meyer. And still hovering in the background was his discarded first wife Minna, who died a few years later. At one time or another each of these women had believed − still believed, even − that he belonged to her alone. None of them dreamt that victory in the mating contest would go to the lanky Cosima von Bülow.

With the birth in 1865 of Isolde, the first child of the union of the twenty-seven-year-old Cosima and the fifty-two-year-old Wagner, the exclusivity of their relationship grew more apparent, until finally, by fuelling Wagner's jealousy, not of her husband but of her father, she succeeded in forcing him into a permanent bond. On the birth of their third child, Siegfried, in 1869, he said to her: 'Fate decreed that you should present me with a son . . . We have been compelled to follow that fate, albeit without understanding it.'

Bülow had now assumed the role of the cuckolded husband, his horns growing ever longer. At the beginning he had watched with amusement as the action unfolded, then adopted an increasingly frigid attitude, until finally, 'after six months of living like a bachelor', he found himself left completely out in the cold. Their common friend Cornelius claimed to have evidence that the transfer of Cosima from Bülow to Wagner had taken place 'with the romantic connivance of the two men', but behind the scenes, as Wagner recorded in his *Annals*, there was a great deal of angry 'gnashing of teeth'.

Indeed, sharing Cosima was easier in theory than in practice — and that they did share her was confirmed by Anna Mrazek, the observant housekeeper, in the course of a paternity suit some time later. Anna gave evidence that when, one day in the summer of 1864, Bülow discovered that his wife and Wagner were in Wagner's bedroom together with the door locked, he had lost control of himself. 'Shouting and screaming,' she stated, 'he threw himself on the floor.' A nervous breakdown followed, accompanied by various psychosomatic disorders which made his life a living hell. Wagner, who had just fathered his and Cosima's daughter Isolde, realized that Bülow was facing a state of complete collapse: 'Miserable, almost out of his mind, he is like the insect that is drawn irresistibly into the flame.'

It was an image much to Wagner's liking — he himself as a regal figure who consumed Bülow, the common mortal, as Zeus had once consumed Semele. In Munich, where the adulterous couple and the cuckolded husband afterwards stayed at the King's expense, the chosen imagery was less violent: now Bülow was cast as Menelaus of Sparta, who lost his beautiful wife Helena to Paris. Some also identified him with King Mark in Wagner's own *Tristan*, in which Isolde, Mark's betrothed, is seduced by his nephew Tristan. The neurosis that runs through Wagner's opera spread unchecked into the real world, and Bülow himself, who adored the work, had lovingly made a piano transcription of it and conducted its triumphant premiere in Munich, recognized in it the 'source of the tragedy' that had struck him. 'Would that some pitying soul would give me the dose of prussic acid that I need!' he wrote at the time. Later, in contrast, he was to express his ironical satisfaction that he had not accepted his friend Wagner's 'generous invitation to commit suicide'.

When Nietzsche visited Bülow in Basel in 1872, he was made to feel the rage against Wagner that Bülow had pent up for years. According to Nietzsche's sister Elisabeth, it was a meeting that had 'not been without its embarrassing moments' and in which a number of 'harsh remarks' made by Bülow had caused her brother 'considerable discomfiture'. Only later did the peevish Bülow offer his young guest a somewhat more conciliatory interpretation of the conflict, 'drawing an analogy with classical legend and expressing the triangular relationship in the form of an equation: Cosima = Ariadne, Bülow = Theseus and Wagner = Dionysus.' By means of this mathematical formulation, Elisabeth Nietzsche added, the 'new Theseus' merely wanted to show that he had been succeeded by 'the higher term, the god'. It was an interpretation that Nietzsche had adopted long before his visit to Bülow. As late as 1887 he planned a drama in which Ariadne threatens Theseus with the words 'I shall bring about his downfall': the very situation that Theseus alias Bülow had experienced for himself.

While her husband was forced to withdraw from concert life in Munich on grounds of health, Cosima's activity was reaching new heights. Mother of two daughters by Bülow and two by Wagner — the existence of the latter doggedly ignored by her husband — she became Wagner's private secretary with the authority to act on his behalf — a role known in Munich as that of a 'carrier pigeon' — and embarked on a vigorous campaign to promote his cause. She drew the young King Ludwig, who was passionately in love with Wagner, into an extended correspondence, conducted partly in a formal, French-classical style, partly in the high-flown language of *Lohengrin*, with the sole aim of getting him to lead the crusade on behalf of Wagner's operas. As one way of overcoming the difficulties she even conceived the idea of ingratiating herself with the sceptical Queen Mother by offering to read to her. After a year of such intrigues, however, the King's patience ran out and he restored what he felt to be an appropriate distance between himself and his importunate suppliants.

Long after they had been thrown out of Munich, Wagner and Cosima continued to assure the King that their relationship was merely one between friends. Yet in Tribschen, the villa on Lake Lucerne that Ludwig had financed from his private purse, they lived as man and wife, together with the offspring they hoped to legitimize by their subsequent marriage. But before this could happen, Cosima had to seek a divorce.

So in October 1868, accompanied by Bülow's two daughters Daniela and Blandine, and Wagner's two daughters Isolde and Eva, she set out on her painful journey to Munich to cajole Bülow into dissolving their marriage. But plead and threaten as she might, Bülow had for the moment no intention of complying. In the first place he still loved her; secondly he had no wish to lose his daughters to Wagner as well; and in any case, as he jubilantly pointed out, divorce for a Catholic was out of the question, a view that Liszt, his father-in-law, emphatically confirmed.

Wagner, of course, had foreseen all this and, as he recorded in his *Annals,* had extracted from Cosima a promise that she would renounce her Catholicism, a promise that now plunged her into a state of spiritual crisis. Her father, still at the mercy of the sanctimonious Carolyne von Sayn-Wittgenstein, was living as an abbé in Rome. If she were to persuade him to grant her a dispensation, she would have to make her pilgrimage to the Eternal City. The very idea brought the jealous Wagner to the verge of panic. When he tried to circumvent her journey by seeking the intercession of her half-sister Claire, Cosima flew into a rage and accused him of going behind her back.

Repudiated by the King, at odds with his lover and with no prospect of either Bülow giving way or Liszt granting them his blessing, Wagner adopted a tried and tested strategy for solving problems. He absconded. At the beginning of November he bought a first-class train ticket to Leipzig, there to seek consolation in the company of his family. It was here, one evening, in the house of his brother-in-law Hermann Brockhaus, that his attention was drawn to one of the other guests, a young man who hung on his every word, quoted from his writings by heart and clearly had the ideal qualities to become a novice in the Wagnerian Order of the Future. His name was Friedrich Nietzsche.

3

The Euphoric
Acolyte

Nietzsche visited Wagner's lakeside villa of Tribschen some two dozen times after 1869. Twenty years later, quivering in a no-man's-land between sanity and madness, like a tightrope walker crossing a chasm, he had turned it into Naxos, island of classical legend. Here, according to the myth, Ariadne, deserted by her lover Theseus, was found by Dionysus and shown the way to the celestial regions – analogous, in their way, to the spiral tunnels of the labyrinth.

Nietzsche's extraordinary version of this episode, where, instead of comforting Ariadne, Dionysus drags her along by the ears in a highly uncavalier fashion, appears in his polemical essay *The Twilight of the Idols*, written in the summer of 1888. Here he maintains that this mischievous incident took place in the course of one of those 'famous conversations that Princess Ariadne, alias Cosima von Bülow, used to hold with her philosophical lover, alias Nietzsche, on the island of Naxos'.

Nor was the allusion to Naxos the only moment of mystification through which Nietzsche now drew his distant experience of Tribschen into his Dionysian fantasies. In the autobiographical

Ecce Homo, revealing to the world 'why I am so wise', he returns in his imagination to Wagner's villa in order to carry out further exercises in transfiguration, rhapsodizing in extravagant language on 'the intimate relationship with Wagner' which brought him 'the most profound, the most heartfelt comfort . . . those days of joy and intimacy in Tribschen, those moments of sublime harmony.' 'I know nothing of what others have felt in the presence of Wagner,' he concludes: 'I can only say that no cloud ever darkened the sky above our heads.'

He knew perfectly well that this was not true. But so desperately did he wish it to be that his fevered imagination made him pretend that it was so. Certainly, if not before, then from the time Bülow confided to him the circumstances of his own eviction from the scene, Nietzsche had known 'what others experienced in the presence of Wagner'. He could only have enjoyed those 'days of intimacy' before he realized that Wagner's nature was characterized 'less by trust than by mistrust', as he later wrote. And Cosima, at least, had not noticed much 'joy' during the time they were together in Tribschen. On the contrary, years afterwards she let it be known that the 'poor night-bird', as she called him, had never been joyful, nor had he ever laughed or understood the badinage that passed between her and Wagner.

The sky above them in Tribschen — to retain the meteorological image — was generally overcast and often exploded in a storm, with Wagner hurling down his thunderbolts. Tribschen was never an idyllic place, and one is tempted to think that Nietzsche chose the wrong location for his mythological analogy. More appropriate than the shores of Naxos would have been the impenetrable labyrinth from which the only escape was by the thread that Ariadne held in her hand. But she had other plans for the use of that thread.

From the beginning, 1869, the year the twenty-four-year-old Nietzsche first visited the 'Lord Minotaur' and his mistress in Tribschen, had a fairy-tale air about it. Through the good offices of

Friedrich Ritschl he was appointed professor extraordinary at the University of Basel, with rosy prospects of promotion and at a salary that corresponded exactly to Wagner's rent for Tribschen. On Whit-Saturday he eagerly took the train from Basel to Lucerne, intending to present himself unannounced at the villa. His clothes reflected his new status. He wore a grey felt top hat, and just as his thick professorial glasses contrasted with his military moustache, so his mincing gait seemed at odds with his grim-faced expression. He felt a certain hesitancy about coming because Wagner's invitation was now six months old. But finally he decided to walk out to the promontory on which the house stood, pausing for a while in its shadow and listening to 'an agonizing chord that was repeated over and over'. It was the searing music that accompanies Brünnhilde's cry in the final scene of *Siegfried*: '*Verwundet hat mich, der mich erweckt*' ('He who has awakened me has wounded me'), music that matched the mood of the moment. For Wagner had once more become involved in political matters and stirred up unnecessary trouble for himself.

The emancipation of the Jews in Germany was enshrined in the law. But Wagner chose this moment to reissue his inflamma-tory essay of some twenty years earlier, *Das Judentum in der Musik* (*Music and the Jews*), appending a vicious attack on the popular actor Eduard Devrient and his recently published memoir on the composer Mendelssohn. But his calculation that by arousing anti-Semitic feeling he could divert attention from his compromising family circumstances did not work out — at least, not initially. His friends turned their backs on him. His sister Luise wrote that his pamphlet had saddened her, while Bülow coolly observed that it had 'virtually cut off any possibility that Wagner might reconcile himself with the world'. Wagner was looking forward to the celebrations to mark his fifty-sixth birthday on the weekend after Nietzsche arrived. But Cosima wrote sorrowfully in her diary: 'None of his friends or relatives uttered a word. How unpleasant.'

5 Tribschen, the villa on the shores of Lake Lucerne where Wagner and Cosima lived from 1866 to 1872.

But one did. The Whitsun weekend had proved an inconvenient time, and not until two days later was Nietzsche able to pay his first visit to the residents of Tribschen. Before that he had written his hero a rhapsodic birthday letter. Lamenting that there was scarcely a soul with the capacity to 'grasp Wagner in his totality', he expressed his happiness at being the one chosen 'to see the light' and recognize the presence of genius. Above all, he continued, he sensed in Wagner 'the spirit of a more profound, more spiritual philosophy of life', a spirit that had been 'suddenly lost to us Germans through the arrogant behaviour of the Jews'. He signs himself 'Your most faithful and most obedient disciple and admirer, Dr Nietzsche − Professor in Basel'.

This act of obeisance to Wagner's anti-Semitism was accompanied, however, by a reluctant rejection of Cosima's invitation to attend Wagner's birthday celebrations. How dearly he would have accepted, he wrote, 'if only the tiresome demands of my position did not confine me to my dog-kennel in Basel'. Compared to Wagner's villa, with its boathouse and its view of Mount Pilatus,

Nietzsche's room was indeed a 'wretched hovel', as his sister Elisabeth, who kept house for him, called it. But it was not his obligations in Basel that held him back. 'As a teacher, I could not but decline the invitation,' he confided to his friend Erwin Rohde, 'it was a matter of morality.'

For it was not Wagner's crude anti-Semitism that repelled Nietzsche, the clergyman's son, but his adulterous affair with his mistress, the consequences of which were as obvious to Nietzsche as to anyone else. Cosima greeted her guest from Basel in an advanced state of pregnancy but with no suggestion that the child had been fathered by the man whose name she bore. This was the scandalous situation that led the anxious Nietzsche to fear for his reputation as a teacher and to avoid the couple for a while. He even hid his embarrassment from Elisabeth until the problem could no longer be concealed. 'I gradually came to realize', she wrote, 'that the *ménage* of Wagner and Baroness von Bülow could not but give offence in some quarters.' For a long while Nietzsche even withheld from his sister the news of the birth of Siegfried, the couple's third illegitimate child, so that when she paid her first visit to Tribschen, she was surprised to set eyes on the boy.

The notoriously suspicious Wagner, too, observed that Nietzsche was 'unnaturally reserved', which displeased him all the more because Cosima was constantly brooding over their illicit liaison and cultivating what she called 'the ecstasy of suffering', of which he severely disapproved. After their marriage had finally been solemnized in August 1870 Wagner snidely remarked that nobody was happier to see the legitimization of their relationship than Nietzsche, who had 'suffered intensely' under the irregular situation.

Finding himself increasingly sickened by Basel and the atmosphere of 'repressed idealism' that prevailed there, Nietzsche quickly discarded his spinsterish sensibilities and took his place as Wagner's new sorcerer's apprentice. On his second visit to Tribschen in June 1869, 'in perfect weather and under a blazing sun', as Cosima recorded, he was received with full honours, taking coffee with them in the garden and strolling along the 'Robbers' Path' by the lakeside. The evening was given over to his host's predilection for reading aloud from his own works, in this case from *Music and the Jews*. Here — and not by chance — he could illustrate to his young disciple the two main targets of attack in his programme of cultural renewal. One was the decline of the German language, as exemplified by Devrient's book on Mendelssohn; the other was the Jews. Nietzsche listened in fascination, as he had done in Leipzig, and stored the poisonous message in his mind for future use.

Life at the Wagnerian court in the white villa, set in a magic landscape of mountains and green fields stretching down to the lake, made a deep impression on the young professor. Apart from Wagner and Cosima, with her four daughters, there were a governess and a nanny, together with the housekeeper Vreneli Stocker and her husband Jacob, who later poked fun at Nietzsche's compositions. Finally there were a manservant, a cook and a housemaid. A Newfoundland and a pinscher ran up and down the corridors, while in the stable stood a coach horse called Fritz, soon to be joined by the nag Grane, a gift from King Ludwig. The call of the two peacocks, Wotan and Fricka, could be heard in the garden and, besides rats and chickens, cats and sheep, there were bats — animals that appeared as evil omens to the superstitious Cosima. From time to time the guest rooms were occupied by the Master's acolytes busily copying scores.

In the course of the first night that Nietzsche spent at Tribschen another newcomer arrived, apparently unnoticed by him at the time. 'I learnt later', he wrote, 'that Siegfried was born that night.' Knowing that Cosima was about to give birth, Wagner had at first wanted to cancel Nietzsche's visit but she had insisted. Certain that the young professor was in the habit of quoting from Wagner's treatise *Opera and Drama* in his lectures, she did not want to run the risk, during this period of public ostracism, of losing him as well. They therefore created for him a sublimely artificial Wagnerian world and drew a veil over the real situation.

For a crisis was looming. Jealous of the daughters to whom he accused Cosima of sacrificing herself, Wagner was constantly picking a quarrel. He confined the children to the house and forbade Cosima to continue with her embroidery − 'He thinks it is taking hold of me,' she wrote − all because he could not bear not to be the exclusive centre of attention. Cosima responded by again lamenting poor Bülow's fate and her worries about the unsettled future facing her children. 'Given Richard's inability to moderate his own demands,' she wrote, 'he will not be able to look after them.' When she wrote in her diary 'Foreboding of death', he added alongside it, to her irritation, 'Worried to death'. He was haunted by his old childhood fear of being left alone, a fear that now reached panic proportions when she refused to move into the joint apartment, with adjoining bedrooms, that had been newly prepared for them. 'To have our bedrooms close to each other, as we had originally agreed,' she wrote, 'now that the older children are here as well, would make me feel embarrassed.' Her decision to stay on the upper floor put him in a bitter mood and, taking his pillows and blankets with him, he moved downstairs on his own. It was only a few days before her confinement, and she felt as though he had given her 'the *coup de grâce*'. He, for his part, reflected on the thought that Beethoven had died in his fifty-seventh year − his own age at that moment. Everything pointed to a twilight of the Gods.

Then Nietzsche appeared. Still in a daze, the pregnant Cosima had difficulty in following his words − 'they sounded like an echo from afar' − but did not retire to bed before she and Wagner had spent a convivial evening with the new arrival and bidden him goodnight at around eleven o'clock. Towards three in the morning the midwife arrived and Wagner could no longer bear to stay in his own part of the house. 'Bursting into the room,' we read in Cosima's diary, 'he found me writhing in pain with the midwife

6 Richard and Cosima Wagner in Vienna, 1872, two years after
their marriage.

bending over me. The sight of him suddenly standing there gave
me a shock and I thought I was seeing a ghost. I averted my gaze
in horror, which drove him out of the room.'

It was Wagner himself who recorded in Cosima's diary this
painful scene as viewed through her eyes. He was dumbfounded at
the violent reaction he had provoked. Was it due to her continued
resentment of his irritable outbursts and his constant carping, which

totally demoralized her? Or was she reminded of the birth of her second daughter, Blandine, which, she later wrote, 'almost ended in tragedy as a result of the utter callousness of my mother-in-law', who at the crucial moment had left her in the lurch? Or again, was it the guilt complex she had over Bülow, who she imagined in her hallucination had returned and was now standing before her?

Banished to a side room, Wagner heard the pain-racked cries of Cosima in labour – Nietzsche must have taken sleeping pills not to hear anything. Finally, Vreneli cried: 'It's a boy!' A sense of triumph, a feeling of joy, the bliss of flowing tears – all mingled with the breaking dawn and the sound of the church bells of Lucerne calling the early worshippers to prayer. So overwhelmed was Wagner that he forgot to mention to Cosima that their impromptu guest had left that same day. The guest had in any case made no lasting impression. The one name they did remember was that of his friend Erwin Rohde: while Cosima was in labour, Nietzsche had read to his distracted host the letters in which Rohde declared himself to be an enthusiastic disciple of the Master. After her convalescence, Cosima asked to hear about 'those letters from your friend that you read recently to Herr Wagner'.

Immediately he got back to Basel, Nietzsche told Rohde about the turbulent weekend at Tribschen, adding that he had found his stay 'remarkably stimulating'. As to Wagner himself, he went on, 'he makes all conceivable wishes come true, and the world has not the slightest idea of the greatness of the man or the uniqueness of his personality.' Such exaggerations are partly explained by the fact that after a mere six weeks Nietzsche's professorship had become a burden and the city of Basel 'totally alien and a source of complete indifference', leaving the figure of Wagner as his sole consolation. For the same reason he was prepared to ignore those 'trivial transgressions and peccadilloes which spiteful rumours attribute to him'.

There followed the days of the 'famous conversations on Naxos' between Cosima as Ariadne and Nietzsche as Wagnerian acolyte, the latter as yet uncertain of his role in the myth. The conversations took place against a background of the music of the *Ring des Nibelungen* on which Wagner was working; at all other times Wagner insisted on being the centre of attention. But of those conversations there is unfortunately no record.

Nietzsche's sister, however, recalled one remarkable walk. 'The sun was sinking in the west,' she wrote in flowery language, 'but the full moon had already risen above the clear, snowy slopes of Mount Titlis.' Cosima and Nietzsche walked together by the side of the lake, 'Cosima wore a pink Cashmere gown trimmed with broad lace borders that hung down to meet the hem of her dress; hanging from her arm was a broad Florentine hat with a garland of pink roses' — all, like her expensive dress, reflecting Wagner's love of sumptuous shades of pink and his taste for the latest French creations, which he learnt about from Parisian fashion journals. He himself wore his familiar velvet biretta that evening, with a black velvet cloak and a light blue cravat.

Since Elisabeth's attention was entirely devoted to Wagner during the walk, she could not overhear what the other two were saying, so she tamely concluded her story by having them all fall into a 'wistful silence'. That silence was broken only when they reached the highest point of the garden. Then, Elisabeth continued, 'Wagner, Cosima and my brother began to talk about the tragedy of human life, about the Greeks, about the Germans and about their own intentions and desires.' So impressed was she by what she heard that she claimed never before to have experienced 'such profound harmony between three such different people'. Exactly what had fascinated her she could no longer remember. In Cosima's diaries, which are not above trivialities where the Master's own utterances are concerned, there is not a word about either the walk or the conversation.

The name Nietzsche does, however, occur frequently in these diaries. Often it is misspelt and rarely is the reference as Nietzsche himself might have wished it. Usually he receives only a brief mention, a mere statement of his presence, recorded in a somewhat critical tone appropriate less to the 'friend' he saw himself to be than to a new retainer with a tendency to absent himself without permission. Only on the occasions when he showed himself to be of use, a man prepared to carry the banner that proclaimed the Master's message, do the entries become more cordial. But generally there was just the name, together with his title, to which they attached great importance. A diary entry for the end of July 1869 – by which time they must have known who they were dealing with – records a visit from 'Professor Nietsche [sic], a pleasant, well-educated man'. The following day the man and his title joined them at table and again made a 'very pleasant impression'. Less well received was his remark that Liszt's oratorio *The Legend of St Elisabeth* 'smelt more of incense than of roses' – a remark held to be a slur both on Cosima's father and on her favourite saint. But the 'young dandy', as Wagner later called him, had little idea what these people in Tribschen were really like, and was happy to retain the idealized vision that their amiability encouraged him to cultivate.

Summarizing his impressions of Wagner after his visit, Nietzsche wrote: 'There is a perfection, an absolute greatness about this man's qualities, an ideality of thought and sentiment, a uniquely noble and warm-hearted humanity and a profound sense of the meaning of life which make me feel in the presence of one of the chosen spirits of the age.' At the same time he was in no doubt that Wagner – not a man given to false modesty – shared his assessment and therefore demanded his complete subservience.

'Wagner's whole life is patriarchal in nature,' wrote Nietzsche, the young man who had grown up without a father of his own. He now found himself assigned to the lower ranks of a family hierarchy. The upper ranks were occupied by those he remembered as 'the little Bülow children, Elsa, Isolde, Senta and Siegfried', while in the highest rank of all stood 'the wise and noble Frau von Bülow, a figure fully worthy of these palatial surroundings'. Unreserved in his praise, he summarized his days in Tribschen in one sentence, a remarkable sentence to come from a professional academic. They were, he said, 'without doubt the most valuable products of my time as a professor in Basel'.

Another of his friends, Carl von Gersdorff, received a similarly euphoric description in which Nietzsche raised the pitch of his enthusiasm still further. Emanating from the presence of Wagner, he wrote, was 'an absolute ideality' and 'a sublimity of mind' that made one feel as if one were 'in the presence of the divine'.

Such feelings were intensified by Wagner's essay *Über Staat und Religion (On State and Religion)*, written in 1864, which Nietzsche read during a three-day sojourn in a fog-bound hotel on Mount Pilatus. This politico-philosophical farrago addressed to King Ludwig, which Nietzsche immediately encouraged others to read, testifies less to 'the presence of the divine' than to the author's calculated cunning in telling his young patron what he wanted to hear – namely that he, Wagner, had never, as the shameful accusation charged, been involved in revolutionary politics, and that far from considering progress to be the motive force behind the state, as he had once done, he now saw stability as the pivotal quality, represented by monarchy, of which Ludwig was 'the perfect embodiment and guarantor'. The young King, Wagner went on, needed more desperately than any other ruler the 'spiritual fortification and consolation of religion', a source of strength second only to art. For art, 'the benevolent saviour', 'both lives in life yet raises itself above life, which it presents to us as a game'.

Life turned by art into a game – this was a remarkable concept that may well have stimulated the childlike fantasies of Ludwig's later years. Beyond doubt, however, it was this concept, stimulated by Schopenhauer, of art as 'a play of fantastic images' or as an unfathomable 'divine vision' which rises above the sordid reality of everyday life, that formed the core of what was to develop into

Nietzsche's first work, *Die Geburt der Tragödie aus dem Geiste der Musik* (*The Birth of Tragedy from the Spirit of Music*).

Indeed, Nietzsche's weekend visits to Tribschen became themselves 'a play of fantastic images' in which, in a manner indescribable yet true, as he wrote, his idols Schopenhauer and Goethe, Aeschylus and Pindar appeared before him in living form. 'You must believe me,' he besought Rohde, as though recruiting members for a new sect. He himself wanted to believe – that he had found in Tribschen a new home and in Wagner a long-lost father who, like Wotan and his scion Siegfried, would clear the way to his success and happiness by voluntarily renouncing power in favour of a younger man. For had Wagner himself not taken over from Schopenhauer the dogma of 'self-denial', preaching no longer revolution but renunciation, the Schopenhauerian renunciation of 'will' and 'illusion', of eating meat and of vivisection, and – as his *Parsifal* would later teach – of the sinful attractions of the female sex?

In contrast to his Wotan, who renounces all, Wagner did not want to renounce anything. Not only did he continue to enjoy steak and sundry mistresses, he also clung to his plan to found his own cultural empire. After suffering a débâcle in Munich, he was now banking on Bayreuth. Victory would only be his in a place that belonged to him and where he ruled. To this end he needed assistants, supporters, disciples – experts in the art of self-denial. Nietzsche, who was considered in Tribschen to be admirably suited to such a role, persisted in his image of Wagner as father figure. Quoting from Goethe's *Faust*, he called him his 'Pater seraphicus', the figure who had initiated him as one of the 'holy infants' into 'the hidden mysteries of art and life', and paid homage to him as his deliverer 'from darkness into light'. Wagner's birthday, he maintained, marked the celebration of his own birth, and the 'desire to gratify him', he wrote to Rohde, his fellow Wagnerian, 'impels me more powerfully than any other force'.

He also found himself growing closer to the other ruler in the house. In her usually very detailed diaries, dominated by the presence of the Master, Cosima wrote on 3 January 1870: 'No entries for a whole week. Spent most of the time with Prof. Nietzsche, who left yesterday.' Nietzsche himself, usually given to superlatives when describing his visits to Tribschen, had little more to report about that Christmas week, adding in a letter to Rohde only that it had been 'one of my most cherished and uplifting memories'. 'You too', he urged his friend, 'must be initiated into this magical world.'

Had he perhaps fallen victim to Cosima's Parisian attractions? Was he fascinated by her French accent and her dark, low voice, or by the vivacious way she tripped from one subject to another with a brash confidence that made him forget his intellectual superiority? Some ten years earlier, the German socialist Ferdinand Lassalle, a friend of Bülow's, had left a somewhat different account of Cosima's conversational charms. 'She had an obsession,' said Lassalle, 'based on an education the equivalent of that to be had at a French academy for young ladies, with trying to play the intellectual. She got on my nerves.' Nietzsche, however, never tired of her conversation.

But she expected something in return. In 1869, making preparations for Christmas, she asked him to get her a copy of Dürer's engraving *Melancolia* and the sets for a puppet show, which she asked him to set up in the drawing room. After Father Christmas had given the children their presents, the proceedings were dominated by the Master and his reminiscences. A portrait of his uncle Adolph had been laboriously acquired with Nietzsche's help, together with an old almanac containing *Der Bethlehe-mitische Kindermord* (*The Massacre of the Innocents*), a comedy by his stepfather Ludwig Geyer, which he recited to the company on Christmas Eve. The following evenings he read excerpts from his memoirs, after spending the days working on the Prelude to

Götterdämmerung and on the treatise *Über das Dirigieren* (*On Conducting*). This left him in a state of exhaustion and forced him to withdraw, leaving affairs in the hands of the young newcomer from Basel.

With her thirty-second birthday on 24 December forced to take second place to Wagner's domination of the proceedings, Cosima found herself with time to devote to her guest. Indeed, from the very first evening of his visit, when Wagner set about reading Geyer's old potboiler, Nietzsche made a deeper impression on her than before. In earlier months, according to Richard DuMoulin Eckart, her biographer, she had been put off by his 'doctrinaire tendencies' but now, in the Christmas atmosphere and stimulated by Geyer's play, she came to know him better.

The next day, after lunch, they ventured together into the world of the Holy Grail. While Wagner took a nap, Cosima fetched the unpublished draft of *Parzival* (as it was first spelt), the Master's aesthetico-religious last testament, and read it to Nietzsche. Written for Ludwig in one of the King's mountain chalets in 1865, the text was also linked in its own way to Wagner's love for Cosima. Liszt had invited her and Bülow in August of that year to attend the first performance of his *Legend of St Elisabeth* in Budapest, leaving the madly jealous Wagner alone. Forgetting his other mistresses, the deserted Master had sought refuge in art, finding comfort for a while in the story of Parzival.

That moment when Cosima read to Nietzsche from Wagner's draft, reminding her of that poignant episode in the past, was not without its piquancy. Here was a story that told of the 'pain of seduction', of 'the hidden demon of sin and guilt', of 'beautiful creatures in skimpy, provocative attire' − in short, it stimulated all the thoughts that might flash through the mind of a lonely professor in the company of a lady. The erotic suggestiveness reached its culmination in an attempted seduction in which 'the last flicker of maternal longing' merged into 'the first kiss of love'.

Told thus by an adulterous young mother sitting among the silks and satins of a luxurious drawing room, alone with an inhibited young admirer, it was a *risqué* tale, the more so because in the end the hero redeems the sinful king and accedes to his throne. 'Read *Parzival* with Prof. Nietzsche,' she afterwards wrote in her diary: 'again a frightening experience.' The last inhibited young man to whom she had tearfully confided her emotion over *Parzival* had been King Ludwig, whom Wagner privately called 'Parzival'. When the Master returned from his afternoon nap, after Cosima had finished reading, he intimated 'in the most cordial manner', as Nietzsche proudly wrote to Rohde, 'the special role for which he had singled me out'. Maybe he cherished a secret hope that it might be the role of Parzival himself, 'the guileless fool', heir apparent of the kingdom of the Grail.

Cosima too had turned the head of the unworldly young bookworm, writing to him of the 'mood of melancholy' that had prevailed since his last visit and of her conviction that he would bring her luck. A comparison between the intimate tone of these letters and her diaries of the same months, however, presents a different picture. In the latter she records that, far from 'bringing her luck', he arrived with bad news about a newly published book 'devoted entirely to the defamation of R.' Her sadness when he left, she went on, lay therefore not with him but with the man he had left behind: 'What a lonely existence R. is fated to lead in this world.' The professor from Basel was a poor consolation. Shortly afterwards we find Wagner meditating on having discovered his ideal companion. 'I have found my true destiny in the company of this companion,' he told Cosima. But the companion was not Nietzsche – it was Goethe.

Nietzsche, however, convinced that he had found his destiny in Tribschen, now felt sufficiently sure of himself to introduce his own companion into the company. In June 1870 he brought Erwin Rohde with him for the first time, a young friend who had long felt for Wagner an admiration and reverence 'bordering on the

religious'. Two years earlier Nietzsche had confided to Rohde his
jubilation over Wagner's music, adding: 'I have a burning desire to
share my joy with a friend like you.'

The two friends made a considerable impression. 'We are
indebted to you for two glorious days,' Nietzsche later wrote to
Tribschen, 'though for me they were actually four, because
everything my friend Rohde feels, I feel also, thus doubling my
pleasure.' In her reply Cosima expressed her delight that they had
enjoyed their stay and suggested that in future they should always
come together, for the Master himself − 'our liege', as she called
him − had declared that 'man is at his best when two are as one'.

It was a relief for Nietzsche to know that Wagner and Cosima
accepted him on these terms in this delicate area. Wagner, who had
studied classical antiquity since his schooldays, was well aware of
this form of love, which he described to her as an emotion 'which
we cannot conceive and which, provided it did not descend into
depravity, embodied aesthetic ideals at their most sublime'. It was
against such a background that Nietzsche, who felt complete only
when accompanied by his partner, presented himself in Tribschen
− a latter-day Athenian obsessed with art, seeking through his
writing and teaching to bring about under Wagner's auspices a
revival of the culture of antiquity. 'The adoration of woman', added
the Master, for the benefit of Cosima, 'is a completely new
phenomenon which radically divides us from the classical world.'

After the two Dioscuri had left, Cosima wrote to thank them
for a present they had brought with them: 'Dürer's *Melancolia* is a
pleasant reminder of your last visit. It has set the tone for many of
our conversations.' She had asked Nietzsche for the Dürer
engraving at Christmas but only in May had Rohde managed to
find a copy in Venice. An original print would have cost between
400 and 500 francs. The two friends agreed that a copy costing just
18½ francs − 'including postage', as Rohde pointed out − would
serve the purpose. No one at Tribschen seemed to notice.

4

Lessons in Subjugation

The melancholy angel of Dürer's etching now found a place in Nietzsche's private mythological world. Feeling an affinity with the enigmatic creature, he wrote a poem in which he assumed the role of the pensive figure, identifying her with his own Ariadne, goddess of Tribschen, who had been so anxious to possess the picture. He had long observed that she persistently tormented herself with thoughts of guilt and filled her diaries with pointless self-accusations. 'I was made to realize in the cruellest way', wrote the penitent sinner, 'that all our misdeeds will be avenged and that by inflicting this punishment on myself I have become an instrument of the inexorable power of justice.'

Cosima had lighted on this image of the victim that becomes her own instrument of torture – Nietzsche returns to it in his poem 'Ariadne's Lament' – in August 1869 at Tribschen. From the house she could look out over the lake as Dürer's brooding angel casts her melancholy gaze over the desolate watery scene. Looking down mockingly from above is a bat – 'herald of inescapable suffering', as Cosima described the creature to

Nietzsche – while the listless figure herself sits hopelessly entangled in a labyrinth. 'The greater my pain,' she wrote in her diary, 'the stronger this peculiar passion for suffering becomes'. The stronger too – though she kept this to herself – became her passion to cause suffering to others. Houston Stewart Chamberlain, one of her later admirers, described how well she understood the 'art of chastisement'.

Wagner had his own experience of this. Though twenty-four years her senior, he feared her censure like a child and endured agonies when she exacted penance from him for his frequent misbehaviour by refusing to allow him into her bed. In one of the many nightmares in which she tormented him, her father also appeared and made as if to kill him 'with an instrument of torture'. Cosima herself, later describing her part in the dream, 'looked at him coldly, then withdrew into the adjoining room, having been ordered by my father to guard the door'. Horrified by her treachery as an accomplice to his murder, he woke with a piercing cry.

For the young Nietzsche, the realm of dreams and 'the horror of the abyss' were inseparably linked with music. In his poem 'To Melancholy' ('An die Melancholie') the angel soars upwards from its brooding lethargy, a sadistic divinity set on instilling fear into him, causing him to shiver at the sight of its 'terrible features' and shudder when it raised its 'threatening hand'. But his fear and trembling were miraculously transformed into a quivering incantation, the pulsating invocation of 'rhythmic patterns' which appeared on the manuscript paper before him. And if there was a piano available – as there may well have been in that mountain hotel in the summer of 1871, where he was overwhelmed by Dürer's *Melancholia* – he would give himself over to hours of improvisation, leaving the others to listen in amazement to 'the solemn sounds of polyphonic outpourings'. 'He played', wrote one, 'with an immense range of expression, and his intensity made a profound impression on all who heard him.'

It was not in composition — about which Wagner maintained Nietzsche knew less than he thought — that Nietzsche's musical gifts showed themselves, but in improvisation, the extempore translation into musical sounds of passing moods of ecstasy and melancholy. Since his time at Schulpforta, when, following Ortlepp's lead, he used to entertain his friends with his 'wonderful inventions', he had enjoyed the reputation of being a virtuoso improviser, playing with a sense of abandon that had also become legendary in Basel. Once seated at the keyboard, he could not be dragged away from it. 'He is totally oblivious to his surroundings,' wrote one of his colleagues; 'he rhapsodizes on and on and the disgruntled guests have no choice but to leave him to his own resources.'

After a hesitant start, his thoughts would soon begin to flow and with what his friend and follower Heinrich Köselitz (alias Peter Gast), himself a composer, called 'technical perfection' he modulated from one set of strange harmonies to another. 'He had a powerful touch,' said Köselitz , 'yet without being harsh, and his playing was eloquent, contrapuntal in style, with great variations of dynamics.' Already in these early days Nietzsche the composer attracted considerable scorn; it seems that to do him justice one had to hear him improvise at the keyboard.

And this Cosima did. When the Master took a break from composing and went for a walk with his dogs, Tribschen's young visitor was allowed to touch the hallowed keys. He impressed her with his full-blooded performance of the preludes to *Tristan und Isolde* and *Die Meistersinger*, merging without a break into one or other of his own compositions. Cosima found his pieces suspiciously like Schumann's but could not help applauding him for the enthusiasm of his performance. And she soon discovered another, quite different spiritual affinity between them. Nietzsche quickly worked himself into a frenzy while he was playing, arousing in Cosima, herself not unacquainted with states of trance, a familiar 'sense of hallucination, of intoxication'. He had been driven by a state of 'inner turmoil', she wrote later, induced by the 'crushing impact' of Wagner's music, and the longer he played, the tighter she felt 'gripped by a sense of fear and trembling'.

Nietzsche's tendency to hallucinate – on one occasion his landlord, a recent victim of cholera, had suddenly appeared behind his chair, on another, a moaning figure in the throes of death – was exacerbated by his frenzied performances at the keyboard. The superstitious Cosima records a number of episodes in which they tried together to move tables or invoke musical 'oracles', Nietzsche conjuring up the underworld at the piano and increasing her susceptibility to the forces of the occult. At a seance some time later in his apartment in the house of the Bayreuth bookseller Giessel, he was improvising in a darkened room on his *Manfred-Meditation* when, to the consternation of Rohde, who was daydreaming on the sofa, a voice suddenly cried out: 'There's a spirit coming!' But Rohde was too confused to see anything of such an apparition.

Nietzsche must have quickly realized that his performances at the piano gave him a trump card, one that he could play against Cosima no less than against Wagner. For immeasurably greater as Wagner was as composer and poet, he was far from being a born virtuoso – and knew it. Carl von Gersdorff recalled him saying in jest that he played the piano 'like a rat plays the flute'. This shortcoming of Wagner's made Nietzsche feel superior. After playing a number of Wagner's compositions, arranged as piano duets, with one of his favourite students, he would congratulate his partner by saying that he had played one of the pieces better than Wagner himself – 'although', he added slily, 'the Master has never been a good performer'.

But compared with Cosima's husband Hans von Bülow, let alone with her father Liszt, Nietzsche appeared as little more than an ambitious amateur, and his listeners were too spoilt for choice not to grow weary after a while of what Cosima called his 'musical *divertissements*'. Nevertheless she conducted herself diplomatically on such occasions, and when Jacob, the servant, dismissed the guest's performance with the remark, delivered in a broad Swiss accent, 'Don't think much of that', she only smiled behind his back. Wagner, for his part, was as gruff as ever. He could not tolerate the presence of other gods, and certainly not of a professor besotted with music. 'You play too well for a professor, Nietzsche,' he once said spitefully. The latter probably took it as a compliment.

Nietzsche willingly surrendered to any illusion that strengthened his ego. At the Music Festival in Mannheim in 1871, which helped to raise funds for the Festspielhaus in Bayreuth, he imagined himself as having been honoured 'to escort Frau Cosima on her first appearance before the public'. But her detailed account of the Festival makes no mention of any such event. On a similar formal occasion in Bayreuth in 1872, he thought himself the object of particular flattery, whereas in fact people were only sniggering at him. 'The convivial evening was rounded off with a fine banquet *en plein air*', he told Gersdorff proudly, 'at which Frau Wagner and Fräulein Meysenbug were the only ladies present. I was given the place of honour between them and christened Sargino, "pupil of love", after the character in the opera.' Had he actually known Paër's '*dramma eroicomica*' *Sargino, ossia l'allievo dell' amore*, Nietzsche would probably have forgone the allusion, for the hero of this now forgotten work is a snivelling little simpleton who is afraid of his father and apparently also of his horse, which perpetually throws him, and who becomes the laughing stock of the ladies. The only guest present who is likely to have known the work was Wagner himself, who had studied Paër's works in Würzburg in 1833 and now took malicious pleasure in making fun of the solemn young professor.

Another nickname given to Nietzsche was Anselmus, hero of E.T.A. Hoffmann's fairy tale *Der goldene Topf* (*The Golden*

Pitcher), a gauche young man who trips over apple baskets and whose general clumsiness makes him a butt of ridicule. Wagner recited Hoffmann's tale during the Christmas celebrations of 1870 – the famous occasion when the Siegfried Idyll was first performed in the hall at Tribschen. With Wagner himself cast as the magician Archivarius Lindhorst in the story, and Cosima as the beautiful Fire-Lily, the only role left for Nietzsche was that of Anselmus, a factotum competent only to copy the manuscripts in Lindhorst's library, whose daydreams melt into thin air. After Nietzsche had left, 'Archivarius Lindhorst' and the 'Fire-Lily' wrote to 'the student Anselmus' to assure him that he was very welcome to 'trip over more apple baskets' in the future, if he were so inclined.

Basel too, where people valued him as a sympathetic teacher while tittering behind his back at his oddities, turned out to be another of the illusions that cost Nietzsche dearly. His migraines became chronic and his insomnia made him dependent on chloral. The fact that coupled with his professorship at the university was a teaching position at the Gymnasium, overtaxed his strength from the beginning and, since he received only a modest stipend, he was continually worrying about money matters.

In his final semester at the University of Leipzig he had complained about that mysterious spectre 'who had appeared behind my chair' and almost driven him mad with 'the terrifying sound of his hoarse, ghostly voice'. Now, after six strenuous months in Basel, he reported on a new diabolical creature that plagued him – 'the demon of work . . . who will lay violent hands on me before he himself falls into the clutches of the Devil.' Cries for help went out to his friends, telling them he had had to overwork himself for months, not only as a professor but also as 'a hack of a schoolteacher'. If one were to believe his letters, and subsequently his biographers, one would assume that Nietzsche's escape to the idyllic peace of Tribschen brought him the

7 Nietzsche as professor of classical philology at the University
of Basel, 1873.

refreshment of mind and body that he needed. In reality, it only
reduced him to another form of subjugation, one as disastrous to
his fragile self-esteem as the drudgery of his work in Basel had
been to his health. In Tribschen the young professor was to learn
the art of subjugation.

The first commandment of this art was: Fulfil thy every task,
be it never so degrading. By idealizing his visits to Tribschen,
Nietzsche succeeded in obscuring the fact that he had been

relegated to the level of a slave. The price he had to pay for permission to enter Lindhorst's magic kingdom was, as he well knew, the sacrifice of his own personality; and should the pressure of his obligations cause him to forget this, the insistent Cosima was on hand to remind him. Readers of her extensive correspondence, which she later destroyed as far as she could, have maintained that there existed between her and Nietzsche a relationship as between equals. But this overlooks that the occasional intimacies vouchsafed to him by the 'Mistress' − as she liked to call herself in his presence − were calculated solely to put him in a compliant mood. Such superficial gestures were part of an ideological softening-up process aimed at ensuring that the faithful vassal was conditioned to obey the directives issued by the Wagnerian court.

The plethora of missives with which the royal couple bombarded their correspondents followed a division of labour. While Cosima was responsible for sending pleas and warnings to the local authorities, whom, despite her generally informal tone, she always addressed in her capacity as royal spokeswoman, he, the King, concentrated his attention on old friends and patrons, occasionally also approaching new members of his retinue, like Nietzsche, with special requests or demands. His style, at one moment tortuous and obsequious, at the next brash and forthright, was perfectly imitated by Cosima in her own letters, often down to the flowery handwriting. From the conversational tone of an eager adolescent, which found an echo in Nietzsche's heart, she would suddenly affect the imperious manner of a royal consort, which drove him to take flight.

There was no shortage of royal finance or of domestic servants for Tribschen, nor had there ever been a need for an academic errand-boy like Nietzsche. But Wagner and Cosima found in the self-centred young philosopher a ready victim of their policy of using others for their own ends. And at that moment the end bore the name 'Bayreuth'. They used him, for example, to help locate the portrait of Wagner's uncle Adolph, which meant that he had to go to Leipzig, trace the whereabouts of the owner, the deceased uncle's former maidservant, then pester her with a mixture of entreaties and menaces to part with it to Cosima. In the event Nietzsche had the sense to put the commission in the hands of his sister Elisabeth.

From time to time he was employed to cut out newspaper articles and send statements on Wagner's behalf to Leipzig papers. Then, shortly before the Christmas of 1869, he received a mass of more-or-less urgent requests, among them one to arrange for Wagner's volumes of the classics to be rebound in Basel – 'the Greeks in sienna, the Romans in yellow ochre, marbled paper with leather spine, the paper tinted white or yellow with a small pattern, the authors' names on small, coloured labels'. One can just picture Nietzsche standing awkwardly in the bookbinder's shop, peering at the list of Wagner's instructions in his hand. After that he was required to go to the toy shop in the Eisengasse and hand in 'the enclosed note', then to a clothing store, where he was to select some 'tulle with gold stars or polka dots': if the store had no tulle, instructed Cosima in a separate note, he should buy tarlatan – she needed these materials, she explained, for the dress of the Christ child in the manger, and they were 'nowhere to be found in the whole of Lucerne'. And please, she concluded, do not forget to buy a water jug and four glasses, and figures for the Punch and Judy show, including Punch himself, of course.

His next commission involved fresh embarrassments. Wagner, a man with an unerring eye for the most extravagant and expensive detail, had set his mind on possessing a lamp designed by the architect Gottfried Semper, a comrade from the revolutionary days of 1848, with whom, however, he had since fallen out over plans for an opera house in Munich. Nietzsche was sent into the firing line with the task of acquiring this precious item. Pretending to be acting for an unnamed 'lady of rank', he learnt from Semper that a special set of circumstances attached to the piece. It had been consecrated for use in the Dresden synagogue — of which Semper was the architect — by the 'bachelors of the Jewish congregation': consequently, the only ones who could help in the matter were the council of the Elders of Israel or the Jewish jewellers Meyer & Noske, who had manufactured the lamp — all people whom Wagner had recently described as 'a veritable pestilence'.

Wagner was nevertheless determined to have his lamp. Cosima was afraid of compromising herself if she were to order 'a Jewish artefact', so the faithful 'Herr Professor' was again pressed into service. 'May I trouble you again?' she asked. 'I would prefer not to sign my letter to Meyer & Noske with my own name or to send it from Lucerne.' She therefore gave Nietzsche the order for the lamp 'as written and signed by the governess at Tribschen', so that he could either copy it and send it to Dresden under his own name or forward it as it stood, just adding his address. He chose the former course. The affair is only casually referred to in Cosima's diaries: in January 1870 she mentions receiving a sketch of the lamp from Semper, then enlisting the help of Wagner's friend in Dresden, Dr Anton Pusinelli, and finally successfully concluding the transaction. On 4 September 1870, the day their son Siegfried was christened, she wrote in jubilation: 'Installation of Semper's lamp celebrated.'

From now on Nietzsche was expected to put his name and his time totally at the disposal of the lord and lady of Tribschen. He was permitted to order for them Dutch herrings and Russian caviar, a dozen rose bushes and 'several pounds of caramels and apricot pâté', and towards the end was even honoured with a commission to order the Master's underclothes. Since most of the shopping lists that he took back with him from Tribschen to Basel have been lost, we can only hazard a guess at the full extent of the extramural activities in which the young professor was made to indulge.

But his expert knowledge was also in demand. As one well

versed in literature, he was urged to put Wagner's extensive library in order and also asked to recommend an experienced scribe to copy one of his manuscripts – the intention being, as Nietzsche recognized at once, that he should take on the job himself. Above all, however, it was hoped to persuade him to engage his literary gifts in what Wagner considered the most pressing task of the moment, and at the same time the supreme test of Nietzsche's devotion, namely, the publication of his autobiography, *Mein Leben* (*My Life*). The first step was to get the firm of Bonfantini in Basel to submit a written estimate of the printing costs. Then, in an act of 'boundless confidence', Wagner handed over to his young disciple 'a bundle of precious manuscript pages' which Cosima had written from his dictation. Nietzsche was to read them through, then prepare them for the printer. There was considerable urgency about this, insisted Wagner, because he wanted to have printed sheets ready for his approval by Christmas – so as to be able, he added ingratiatingly, to present it to 'the noble lady of our house' on her birthday.

Now elevated by his lord and master to the eminence of 'most worthy friend', Nietzsche strove to meet the unfamiliar demands of this new role but soon ran into a barrage of criticism. As the galley proofs had not been properly corrected, the pedantic ruler of the house sent them back in order to demonstrate how sloppily the typesetter and, by implication, Nietzsche himself had done their work. Besides this proofreading, agony for one with such poor eyesight, Nietzsche had to concern himself with the engraving of the coat of arms that Wagner had thought out for himself, in which it was essential that the 'characteristic ruff round the neck of the symbolic vulture' should prevent any confusion between a vulture and an eagle.* Another of his responsibilities was to

---

*Translator's note: The German for 'vulture' is *Geier*. Wagner here plays on the name of his stepfather, Ludwig Geyer, who was alleged from time to time to have been his natural father. See below p. 162

correct the numerous chronological errors in the text and to ensure that the complete work, which was in any case intended only for the eyes of a select few, was produced in a fittingly lavish form – 'dignified and aristocratic', demanded the Master. In June 1870 Wagner solemnly appointed Nietzsche 'guardian' of 'my profoundly Germanic memoirs', not merely while the book was in production but also 'for posterity'.

'Great geniuses are unpredictable and their ways unfathomable to us common mortals,' wrote Nietzsche in his notebook: they need slaves in order to preserve their 'drone-like' existence. Nietzsche had only one genius in mind. And since it was easy to put him under pressure, Wagner constantly complained to him that responsibility for everything 'lay entirely on his own shoulders' and that nobody was available to help him with matters such as the planning of benefit concerts for Bayreuth. Moved by such cries for help, Nietzsche was prepared to put everything aside and rush to offer his assistance. But, at least for the time being, Wagner spurned his young protégé's willingness to sacrifice his professorship to the Bayreuth cause. On the one hand, the Master could share the social kudos of Nietzsche's distinguished position, a position that Nietzsche openly used to promote Wagner's interests. On the other hand, it predestined him, as Wagner and Cosima saw it, to become the controller of the Bayreuth propaganda machine, a kind of cultural representative travelling the length and breadth of the country as the Master's part-time assistant to market the products of the Nibelung industry and editing a Nibelung review or some similar progressive politico-metaphysical journal. From Wagner's point of view, Nietzsche was a useful asset.

The most noble function reserved for him, however, was that of tutor to the young Siegfried. Back in November 1869, with the child still in his cradle, Wagner had envisaged him as being educated by Nietzsche 'wherever Nietzsche held his Chair', while the proud parents would observe from a distance, 'as Wotan observes the education of Siegfried'. So — as Nietzsche could have worked out for himself — it was not he that was destined for the Wagnerian succession but the Master's own son. In Wagner's scheme of things Nietzsche was only to be allocated the thankless role of Mime, the treacherous dwarf whose reward for bringing up Siegfried is to be slain by his pupil. Not, however, that such savageries were yet in people's minds.

Never did Wagner mount such a barrage of false blandishments as when he made Nietzsche aware of this responsibility. Even his oft-quoted remark, that, next to Cosima, Nietzsche had been 'the only benefit that life has brought me', is to be understood only in the context of the letter in which it occurs, which deals with Siegfried. 'We need someone to form a link between him and me,' wrote Wagner, 'a link like that between son and grandson such as only you can provide.' Wagner the father, Nietzsche the son — the letter made it plain for all to see and Nietzsche accepted the flattering analogy at face value. The bigger the boy grew, the more importunate became his father's ingratiating letters. He even launched into paeans of praise for Nietzsche's compositions, which only recently he had branded 'rubbish' in the company of other musicians. 'The boy constantly reminds me of you', he wrote fulsomely in October 1872, 'and fills me with the desire, born of my family pride, to witness the fulfilment of all the hopes I have pinned on you.' He left the young tutor in no doubt about the nature of those hopes: 'He needs you! — the boy needs you!'

Soon the point had to be reached where Nietzsche could no longer blind himself to the fact that his idol, driven by the egoistic interests of his family, was seriously demanding that he resign his professorship in order to become Siegfried's full-time tutor in Bayreuth. As Wagner envisioned it, by the time the Festival opened in the middle of the decade, at the latest, Nietzsche would have taken up his post in charge of the spoilt, effeminate Siegfried and joined the retinue of the royal Bayreuth couple as a servant charged with grooming someone else for the filial position he had coveted for himself. But Nietzsche, who had ambitions to see his name included among the luminaries of the century, had no intention of complying.

Unbeknown to Wagner, however, who was still convinced that he had his vassal firmly under control, shadows were beginning to fall over his disciple's image of him as a flawless Olympian. Cautious reservations found their way into Nietzsche's notebooks, and with a sharp eye he recorded the contradictions that blemished Wagner's character, contradictions that could not be simply dismissed by appealing to the power of his creative personality. The 'Jupiter' he had worshipped in his early days at Tribschen had changed into 'a strange enigma': on the one hand the visionary reformer, on the other deeply compromised as man and artist – the charming host who could turn into a petty-minded, domineering exploiter; a master of subtle nuances, as Nietzsche still hailed him in 1888, who could lapse into crass, boorish behaviour in private life. Above all, here was a 'friend' who seemed to take delight in inflicting pain on the servant who adored him. It was an enigma that Nietzsche sensed he would not be able to solve without the help of others.

Ten years later, after the final break with the Bayreuth clan, Nietzsche described this period of bondage in the imagery of a beast allegory. In the beginning, as he described the scene in *Also sprach Zarathustra* (*Thus Spake Zarathustra*) – his Gospel according to the Superman – he yielded without resistance, as a 'compliant spirit', to a stronger will: 'Thus he knelt down like a camel waiting to receive his apportioned load.' But then, overladen with burdens from Basel and Tribschen, he flees into the 'lonely desert' in search of his own will, casting off his burden and changing into a lion, king of beasts. Before he can become a true ruler, however, he must overcome the 'glittering gold dragon' that waits to ambush him, as Fafner lies in wait for Siegfried. But the outcome of the fight between the 'Thou Shalt' of the dragon and the 'I Will' of the lion is never in doubt — though this has less to do with his ambivalent relationship to Bayreuth than with the triumphant message of his heroic Superman.

The myth of Dionysus and Ariadne has its own version of this struggle for supremacy. Theseus, with the courage of a lion, advances into the dark tunnels of the labyrinth to pit his heroic strength against the Minotaur. But he owes his victory over the murderous monster not to his own strength but to the love of the Princess, who reveals to him the deadly mysteries of the labyrinth. Nietzsche too, caught up in his own struggle in the Wagnerian labyrinth, could only hope to find his own Ariadne, a figure to help him escape from the impenetrable darkness and from the 'lonely desert' of his doubts. But there seemed no sign of such a figure.

5
'Will Dionysus Flee
from Ariadne?'

Nietzsche's earliest attempt to solve the enigma that was Wagner and at the same time clarify the role played by Cosima alias Ariadne took the form of a drama, planned between 1870 and 1871, on the philosopher Empedocles. Passed over by scholars, the sketches he made for this work were regarded as a 'kind of self-portrait' or, as his biographer Curt Paul Janz put it, a 'persona' in which he appeared 'as he wished to see himself'. One can generally find Nietzsche himself lurking behind his mythological figures. But not in this case. Written during his traumatic experience as a medical orderly during the Franco-Prussian war, the sketches centre not on Nietzsche himself but on a god-like figure who despairs of the world and burdens himself with a deep sense of guilt. The work reaches no conclusion, breaking off in mid-stream like the Kleistian short story that he began at the same time.

Born in Agrigentum, Empedocles had already become a legendary miracle-worker and magician during his lifetime, and is subsequently remembered rather for leaping into the crater of Etna than for his life and his philosophy. An adherent of the doctrine of the transmigration of souls, he stood above the antithesis of life and death, presenting himself as a soul incarnate in youths and maidens alike, transcending the sexes. Inseparable from him in the legend is his young friend and disciple Pausanias, a key character in Hölderlin's drama *Der Tod des Empedokles* (*The Death of Empedocles*), who, after his master's death, 'retrieves his iron shoes, which the volcano has thrown up from the raging depths'. When he died in the fourth century BC, whether in the flames of Etna or, as historians tend to believe, in exile, Empedocles was sixty — just two years older than Wagner at the time the twenty-seven-year-old Nietzsche was planning his drama.

It seems probable that Nietzsche was introduced to Hölderlin's play as a schoolboy by the dissolute philosopher and poet Ernst Ortlepp, who later fell to his own death — albeit only in the gutter. 'When a man so moves the masses,' wrote Hölderlin, 'it is even more terrifying than when Jupiter strikes the forest with a thunderbolt.' This was Nietzsche's world, a world dominated by a god-like figure whose prophetic words were received by the masses 'as a message from Olympus'. In an essay written in Schulpforta when he was seventeen, he described Empedocles' death as an act of 'divine pride, of contempt for humanity, of *taedium vitae*', and sensed in *The Death of Empedocles* 'the years of madness in a living grave' that awaited the unhappy Hölderlin — a presentiment of Nietzsche's own fate.

Ten years later, a welcome guest in a new Olympia among the Swiss mountains, Nietzsche gave his new idol Wagner the name Jupiter. Empedocles came to embody for him the philosophy of pessimism that governed Aeschylus' tragedies and Wagner's music dramas. Like Wagner, Empedocles attributed to himself Titanic powers through which he could overturn society, destroy the ungodly tyranny of science and reason and return to the chthonic mysteries of our origins. But when Empedocles, the 'pan-Hellenic reformer', seeks to offer the Agrigentines a new mythology of 'love, democracy and communal property', he fails — as Wagner was to fail with his revolution under the banner of 'pure humanity' — and becomes for Nietzsche the prototype of the unsuccessful revolutionary.

But what remains if the gods have been destroyed and there is no metaphysical consolation to ease the sufferings of humanity? Answer: Only art, the art of the music drama, the invocation of Dionysus, god of intoxication and abandon, creator of a vision that lifts man above his fear of death and his abhorrence of civilization. Empedocles becomes for Nietzsche the prophet of the state of ecstatic joy, the incarnation of human love, the first to grasp the pure essence of sexual love and point to 'the universal sexual urge' as the driving impulse in the world. And in Wagner Nietzsche found the reincarnation of Empedocles in dramatic form.

Recovered from a disease that almost took his life, still suffering from nervous attacks and memories of 'never-ending moans' from the battlefields, Nietzsche returned from the war and began work almost at once on a first draft of his drama. Cast as a tragic hero who has overthrown the old gods and in return been proclaimed king — 'He is offered the crown by the fairest woman in the land' — Nietzsche's Empedocles is made to watch his city ravaged by an outbreak of the plague while his people begin to harbour doubts about his omnipotence. He thereupon calls for 'spectacular Dionysian bacchanals' — shades of Wagner's Bayreuth to come — a response that anticipates the basic thesis of his treatise *The Birth of Tragedy from the Spirit of Music,* published a year later. The only escape from 'the plague of life', runs this thesis, is through tragedy, in which man becomes aware of 'the terrors of existence' and is at the same time, in his Dionysian stupor, lifted above them. Life finds its justification in the 'god-like vision of art' which is vouchsafed only to someone in this state of ecstasy.

But it is a path to salvation open only to the few. A small élite will find liberation through Dionysian art, but the masses can look forward only to a life of sullen endurance, reaching its end in pain and suffering, at the blind mercy of what Schopenhauer called the Will — the metaphysically irrational and ethically wicked world-purpose heedless of human fate.

Filled with pity, but also consumed with a loathing for life, Empedocles has recourse to a radical answer which comes like a bombshell in Nietzsche's dramatic fragment. 'Empedocles resolves', he writes, 'to liberate the people from their anguish by destroying them in the course of a funeral rite.' They would thus be freed not only from the plague but from life itself, and with it from the curse of the senseless Schopenhauerian Will. In mass destruction alone lies absolute salvation.

Such destruction fantasies, coupled with calls for a 'resolute opposition to everything degenerate and parasitic' and with visions of the destruction of life as 'the mark of a superior class of beings', have been interpreted as symptoms of Nietzsche's madness. But the signs are already present in his *Empedocles*. Moreover, the concept of salvation through destruction comes not from Empedocles but from the one-time anarchist Richard Wagner. Since the abortive coup in Dresden in 1849 Wagner had dreamt of burning down cities and destroying modern mass civilization as part of his attempt to impose his ideal of classical man. Out of the ruins of a degenerate society would emerge his tragic 'culture of the future', just as later Nietzsche foretold that the downfall of the 'last man' would coincide with the triumph of the Superman.

The Dresden uprising failed and a warrant was issued for Wagner's arrest as one of the ringleaders. He fled to Switzerland, where his destructive urge found another outlet — this time that group of people he held principally to blame for the ruin of society and in particular for the decline of musical standards, namely the Jews. In his essay *Das Judentum in der Musik*, first published in 1850, he claimed that only by the elimination of this racial minority, already the object of extensive discrimination, could the way be cleared for the emergence of a new, truly humane culture. He at first concealed this goal behind the metaphor of 'the fall of Ahasverus'; later, when anti-Semitism had become acceptable in society, he called it 'the grand solution', after which there would be no Jews left. Nietzsche's Empedocles, wearing the features of Wagner, is made to utter a similar thought: 'He resolves to destroy the people because he recognizes that they are beyond redemption.'

But the real subject of the drama is the tragedy that Nietzsche witnessed for himself at Tribschen – the tragedy of Cosima's betrayal of Hans von Bülow, culminating in Bülow's downfall and Wagner's triumph. As Wagner assumes the role of Empedocles, so Cosima plays Corinna, 'most beautiful of women', who bestows the crown on the god-like philosopher, with Bülow as Pausanias, Empedocles' favourite pupil. When Corinna learns that Pausanias, to whom she is betrothed, is stricken with the plague, she makes to join him, but to her surprise Empedocles, jealous of his younger rival, now declares his love for her and prevents her from leaving. Confessing her passion, she yields to him. Pausanias perishes to the accompaniment of blood-chilling curses while Empedocles, conscious of his guilt, throws himself into the glowing volcano.

In order to ensure the effectiveness of his heavily intellectualized work on the stage – he was, after all, competing with Wagner's music dramas – Nietzsche settled on the well-proven technique of a play within a play. And no story lent itself better to this treatment than that of Dionysus and Ariadne, the setting of which – the shore of the island of Naxos – recalled the adulterous scene of Tribschen, by the side of Lake Lucerne. Corinna would play the role of the Princess who guided her lover Theseus alias Pausanias through the labyrinth, only for him to abandon her for some inscrutable reason. Empedocles, as king, had ordered the tragedy to be performed, assigning to himself the role of the god.

But with the citizens of Agrigentum gathered in front of the stage, events now take an extraordinary turn. Scarcely has Theseus departed than Empedocles, wearing the mask of Dionysus, appears. Instead of turning to the languishing Princess, he addresses the audience, proclaiming his apocalyptic message of death and rebirth. An uncontrollable fit of frenzy sweeps through the theatre. What began as a play becomes a 'Dionysian bacchanal'.

The jealous Empedocles chooses this very moment, as he reveals himself to his people and is ecstatically hailed as their god – maybe Nietzsche had the triumph of Wagner's *Tristan* in 1865 in mind – to have Pausanias, his favourite disciple and Corinna's lover, murdered. In the first draft, Pausanias dies of the plague; now he is perversely sacrificed to the desires of the philosopher of renunciation. 'Enigmatic revelation of Empedocles' evil lust for destruction,' wrote Nietzsche in his notebook, with the enigma of Wagner before his eyes.

Nor is Nietzsche prepared to leave it there. Divine fate must be helped on its course. By sacrificing his closest friend to his lust for that friend's betrothed, Empedocles must himself die in retribution. He who claimed to redeem humankind from the tyranny of the Will had revealed himself as the unscrupulous agent of that Will, 'a murderer deserving of everlasting punishment', hoping for 'rebirth after dying in retribution'. As the people flee before him, he climbs to the edge of the crater, Corinna at his heels, and plunges into the streams of lava that the raging volcano hurls at him.

Now Nietzsche introduces another surprise. Here is no Wagnerian love-death, the fate that from *Der fliegende Holländer* to *Tristan und Isolde* unites in death the lovers who cannot be united in life. Empedocles attaches no importance to the sacrifice of the deserted Corinna. As he averts his gaze from her and falls to his death, she utters the mystifying cry: 'Will Dionysus flee from Ariadne?' There is no answer. But Nietzsche leaves no doubt that Empedocles turns his back on her, leaving her to die her own death.

The motivation for this disturbing twist in the action lies in Nietzsche's no less disturbing conception of the female sex. The devotion of a tragic philosopher — in this Nietzsche knew that he was of one mind with most classical thinkers — could not be directed at a woman because there was no equality between the sexes. Only in Empedocles' sudden flush of passion — 'an emotional aberration' Nietzsche called it, a passion kindled not by Corinna herself but by the rivalry between him and Pausanias — could she assume the role of a partner. Nietzsche's philosophical notes from this period also share Plato's disparagement of the 'ludicrous worship of woman', to whom, contrary to current prejudice, nature has assigned one role and one alone: 'Woman is there to produce progeny and thus fulfils her given role by living the life of a plant.' The moment this plant spreads into the world of men, however — take the Trojan war — disaster follows. 'Woman is the root of all evil.'

Did Nietzsche really believe that Wagner shared such sentiments, finding a woman attractive only when he knew he was competing with other men for her favours, abandoning her in the instant when his attempt at seduction seemed on the point of success and leaving her with the feeling of having been spurned? In Nietzsche's poem 'Ariadne's Lament' the feared Dionysus takes flight at the very moment when what his love-torn victim seeks is his devotion. Did Nietzsche really think that Wagner, model for his Empedocles, had such problems with women — Wagner, the man who had achieved fame with passionate love scenes on the stage and could have listed a whole series of his own infamous affairs? Why should such a man, this seductive Dionysus, shrink from women? The answer, which Nietzsche did not pluck up the courage to give until 1888, was — because he was a woman himself.

There can be no doubt but that Wagner had a feminine side which he could hardly conceal from Nietzsche. His love of

extravagant clothes and perfumes, his penchant for plush interiors
in the lavish style captured in the paintings of Makart, above all
his uncontrollable urge, frowned upon by Cosima, to dress up in
ostentatious costumes, including women's gowns and negligées –
all this had led his young follower to draw his own inescapable
conclusions. Besides this, Wagner had an insidious gift for making
young men fall in love with him, which was often taken as an
indication that he had homosexual tendencies of his own. This
seems unlikely. But Wagner evidently felt a need to surround
himself with men who clearly did have such leanings – a
tradition that left its influence on the atmosphere surrounding
Bayreuth during the era of the 'effeminate' Siegfried, long after
his father's death. In 1895, for instance, we find the writer Oskar
Panizza sneering at *Parsifal* as 'pabulum for pederasts' and inviting
audiences to join him in the 'mountain caves of *Venus masculinus*'.
At the Bayreuth Festival of 1909, Alban Berg sardonically refused
to allow 'a sinister procession of homosexual Wagnerians' to sour
his enjoyment of the occasion.

Not until after his break with Wagner did Nietzsche feel driven
to make his knowledge public. 'During his late years,' he wrote in
1888 in *Der Fall Wagner* (*The Case of Wagner*), 'Wagner was
unmistakably *feminini generis*', which leads back, as he noted in
another context, to the bisexual god in his labyrinth, that 'labyrinth
of the modern soul' through which there was no more consummate
guide than Wagner. Poisoning his friends with his 'feminism',
Nietzsche warned, the Wagnerian monster of 'ambiguity' and
'ambivalence' reveals himself as the 'Old Minotaur' into whose
clutches 'columns of the finest youths and maidens' are delivered
year after year 'for him to devour'. By the time Nietzsche wrote
these hate-filled words, his Minotaur had been dead for five years
and the Bayreuth labyrinth was in the hands of Ariadne.

6
The Spirit that
Begets Tragedy

At the time of its publication, *The Birth of Tragedy* cast that same shimmering mystical aura round Nietzsche in Wagnerian circles that, in the years of his insanity twenty years later, was to become his characteristic feature in the eyes of the whole of Europe. Written immediately after the *Empedocles* sketches and published in 1872, it remains, like *Empedocles*, a problematic work. 'It is a study', wrote Giorgio Colli, co-editor of the critical edition of Nietzsche's writings, 'which from a historical point of view still remains largely a mystery.' Nonetheless, scarcely any other of Nietzsche's works reached such a wide public. Its antithesis of Apollonian and Dionysian became part of the vocabulary of cultured conversation, while its reinterpretation of Greek antiquity, which moved beyond the frontiers of orthodox scholarship, culminated in an encomium of Wagner's *Gesamtkunstwerk*. The *Ring des Nibelungen*, said Nietzsche, was a contemporary *Oresteia* – Wagner was Aeschylus reborn and the new German Reich, victorious in the Franco-Prussian war, was the legitimate successor to Athens. Yet, insists Colli, all this does not lead us to the heart of Nietzsche's message, which can only be grasped after a kind of 'initiation' into the successive stages of his visionary world.

Nietzsche himself, who felt urged to publish his own critique of the work in 1886, took a similar view. At the time, he explained, when he had been writing 'in the guise of an academic', his sole aim had been to attract kindred spirits and win them to his cause − not, of course, the cause of a scholar but of 'a disciple of an unknown god'. Initiation into the secrets of this mystic philosophy would take place, not in places of popular entertainment but in the winding paths of the labyrinth, which classical writers had long suspected to be the scene of ritual dances. The dancers would be led through narrower and narrower spirals until they reached the final stationary moment of death, then return whence they had come, back through the ever widening circles of life, to emerge as reborn creatures. Every birth, says the mystic wisdom, is preceded by a death.

This experience of a life-giving death became the secret message of Nietzsche's *Birth of Tragedy*. Conceived, as he wrote in a 'Preface to Richard Wagner', among the 'horrors and glories of the recent war' and developed amid the roar of cannons, it revealed Nietzsche's Dionysian conception of the lord of Hades who is reborn as the god of the joy of life. And only through the destruction of his false social identity will man regain his true nature. As he cries out at the sight of the suffering of the world, so his lamentations turn into a passionate threnody out of which tragedy is born − the story of the sufferings of Dionysus, condemned to a fate of torture and agony in whatever persona he appears. But because he thereby experiences for himself the fate of mortal man, he now appears in a new vision, created in the tragic, agonizing yet ecstatic image of music, transformed into an Apollonian figure embodying the beauty of Aeschylean and Wagnerian drama.

In tragedy, Nietzsche goes on, it is not 'mere theatre' that is at issue but reality itself, the frightening manifestations of which torment mankind as the vulture tortured Prometheus. Recalling his childhood nightmares and the horrors of the war, his existential assumptions undermined by Wagner, god of music, he posits that the world can be understood only as an aesthetic phenomenon and that the meaning of life is to be sought not in man but in art: once human suffering has been transmuted into art, it has served its metaphysical purpose. In this dangerous idea Nietzsche thought he had found the thread that would enable him 'to find his way through the labyrinth that we must identify as the origin of Greek tragedy'.

It was in the first weeks of 1871, the time of the foundation of the German Reich, when he applied for leave from his duties in Basel on grounds of 'insomnia, discomfort from haemorrhoids and nervous exhaustion', that Nietzsche conceived the crucial principle that it was not only in the theatre that reality could be transformed into art. The two worlds of the Apollonian and the Dionysian, he wrote — like Hellenic life itself — served a single purpose, namely, to prepare the way for 'the birth of genius'. Genius, divine creator of art, alone represents 'the goal and the ultimate purpose of nature', which may also have recourse to inhuman means to ensure its emergence — 'for nature, even when striving to produce a thing of beauty, is something terrifying.' Then as now, he goes on, man tortures himself 'by perpetuating the miseries of his miserable existence', blinding himself to the unbearable truth by invoking spurious concepts such as the dignity of man or the dignity of work — feeble illusions of 'a slave society hiding from itself'.

At the same time, antiquity demonstrated that a genuine culture could only flourish through the labours of the toiling masses. 'In order for there to be a fruitful soil for the florescence of art,' wrote Nietzsche, 'the overwhelming majority must serve as slaves in the service of a minority, totally subject to that minority over and beyond the mere necessities of life.' All is built on this foundation — 'servitude is intrinsic to all cultures.'

Thus he compares culture with a 'bloodthirsty gladiator' who binds his conquered victims to his chariot and drags them along with him like slaves — the noblest task that can befall them, the aesthetic justification for their existence, as it were. Nietzsche therefore saw the roots of the social privation of the time — of which he was fully aware — as lying not in slavery but in 'the progressive enervation of modern man', for which the only proven antidote was that provided since the days of classical Athens by nature herself, namely 'servitude, albeit under a gentler name'.

Nietzsche attributed this growing enervation and degeneration of the masses to the spread of an 'optimistic, liberal *Weltanschauung*' behind which he claimed to identify the same element that Wagner had held responsible for the decline of music — the Jews. He chooses to pillory these 'ubiquitous, homeless usurers', whom he does not mention by name, as the source of all social ills and at the same time as obstacles in the path of the ascendancy of German culture, heralded by Wagner's music dramas and by the German victory over France. The only remedy against these 'stateless nomads' who have gained control of the world's finances is 'war, war and war again'.

Nietzsche then launches into a rapturous eulogy of war itself, lauding the warlike Apollo and his 'fearful silver bow', who, as 'the true god of purification and consecration,' will cleanse the land of base usurers with his unerring barbs, 'while everywhere corpses are smouldering on the funeral pyres'.

This macabre fantasy of slavery and murder, most likely prompted by Wagner and written by Nietzsche after his Christmas visit to Tribschen in 1870, was not, as originally planned, included in *The Birth of Tragedy*, but was published subsequently, its barely disguised declaration of war on international Jewry still intact, dedicated to the mistress of Tribschen. 'To Frau Cosima Wagner,' he inscribed it, 'in sincere devotion and as a response to questions raised in conversation and in letters. Written in joy and serenity, Christmas 1872.' The sharp-witted Cosima replied coolly and diplomatically. There were certain things, she told him, that one just did not say, especially not 'in joy and serenity'. 'I cannot imagine saying such things in such a mood,' she said. In her diary she refers with displeasure to his 'uncouth manner', though conceding at the same time the depth of his emotions.

Wagner and Cosima were enthusiastic about *The Birth of Tragedy* when they received it at the beginning of 1872. Admittedly, as Wagner wrote in his letter of thanks, they had noticed for some time 'deeply disturbing features' in his manner which recurred so frequently 'that, in a spirit of true friendship, we felt we should exercise a certain reserve in our dealings with you'. But this feeling vanished the moment the work arrived. 'I have read nothing finer than your book,' Wagner wrote to him with deliberate hyperbole, going so far as to add: 'As I said to Cosima, in my affections you come immediately after her, then – a long way behind – comes Lenbach, who has painted a strikingly lifelike portrait of me.' He evidently recognized himself in the image that emerged from Nietzsche's book, an ideal image cherished otherwise only by his devoted Cosima.

Yet as Lenbach's portrait was soon to fall into disfavour, so also in Nietzsche's book there were things that displeased the Master, such as Nietzsche's laying claim to certain ideas that were in fact his, or an impertinent dedication that described Wagner as 'one of my noble pioneers'. Centre stage, Wagner reminded the young author, was occupied by him, not by his disciple. 'As I stand and gaze with you into the far distance, challenging new fields open up before me – before *me* – while you stand at my side.' The repetition left little doubt as to who was the visionary and who his assistant.

Cosima, however, launched into a paean of praise. 'What a fine book you have written!' she wrote to the assistant: 'How wonderful, how profound, how bold!' – hailing him as 'the greatest source of Wagnerian knowledge'. One more overstatement, after all, was neither here nor there.

The same day that Nietzsche's *Birth of Tragedy* arrived in Tribschen Wagner reallocated the roles in the play. 'He calls me his priestess of Apollo,' wrote Cosima in her diary, 'while he himself represents the "Dionysian element".' The only part left for Nietzsche was that of herald. 'Wagner hopes', noted Cosima, 'to found a journal in Bayreuth with Prof. Nietzsche as editor.' The aim of this journal, which under the name *Bayreuther Blätter* subsequently became a vehicle for the dissemination of Wagner's ideas — Nietzsche's friend Rohde scornfully dismissed it as a 'rag' — was to help achieve the renewal of culture which Wagner also found promoted in Nietzsche's book.

But there was no doubt in Tribschen about the identity of the intellectual progenitor. 'It was my lead that he followed,' wrote Wagner to his nephew Clemens Brockhaus, a friend of Nietzsche's, 'so no one can judge better than I how deeply my ideas have penetrated the mind of this man.' '*My* ideas', emphasized Wagner, and Cosima too never tired of pointing out who the creator of this cultural empire was. When *The Birth of Tragedy* took shape 'almost before our eyes . . . a work virtually created for us', she wrote later, Nietzsche was still 'completely free' of that 'tiresome egocentricity' that later befell him, and regarded his book as the fruit of his study of the Master's writings. 'And since when', she went on, 'have apostles with the talent to put an idea into practice been looked down on as mere mimics? Does it not lie in their very nature that they should feel driven to represent their Master and interpret his message, each in his own manner?'

Wagner was jealous of his intellectual property rights. Even before the appearance of *The Birth of Tragedy* he had made Nietzsche aware that the antithesis of the Apollonian and the Dionysian had already formed part of a vision that had led to the revolutionary essays he had written in Zurich over twenty years earlier. 'Only recently,' he wrote to Nietzsche in November 1871, 'to my great astonishment — as though I had suddenly understood the oracle – my mind turned from Genelli's *Bacchus among the Muses* to your own latest work, in so far as I am acquainted with it. There is a quite remarkable consistency throughout my life which I find demonstrated in the idea you express, starting with this painting.' The painting in question, Nietzsche told Rohde, was a watercolour by the classicist Weimar painter Bonaventura Genelli that hung on the wall in Tribschen. Bacchus, god of wine, and the muses in their Olympian serenity had hitherto been seen as irreconcilable opposites; in Genelli's painting they appear together, demonstrating that the ecstasy of the god of music is inseparably bound to the Apollonian muses. Wagner saw in this a prediction of his *Gesamtkunstwerk*, in which the sisters, wrenched apart by the force of cultural decline, are reunited with their brother, deity of music, to create the new music drama of *Der Ring des Nibelungen*.

It had been back in 1868, while he was still in Leipzig, that Nietzsche had studied for the first time the writings of Wagner that anticipated *The Birth of Tragedy*. The following year, ensconced in his 'charming little room' in the Master's house, with its open views over the lake, he returned to them. What now confronted him, supplemented by Wagner's personal comments, was a political programme culminating not, as in Wagner's Dresden days, in issues like democracy and human rights but in a form of religious drama that celebrated both god become man and man become god. Only Athens at the pinnacle of its glory had experienced such a divine mystery, when the marble figure of Apollo had descended from the temple and become a dramatic hero on the stage, embodiment of 'a true, living art'. 'Such was the vision of great Apollo that appeared before the eyes of the tragic poet held in the thrall of Dionysus,' Wagner had written in Zurich. And such, too, in Wagner's house by the lake, was the vision that appeared to his young disciple, inspired by the power of his Master's thoughts.

8 Wagner in Bayreuth in 1876, the year of the first Bayreuth Festival.

But Athens, where tragedy and a deified humanity had flourished, was no more. The arts, which had formerly worked hand-in-hand to a common end, had gone their separate ways and the theatre had declined from a divine celebration to a mere source of pleasure − symbol of a world deserted by the gods.

At this moment of profound decadence, Wagner sought, in the rebirth of tragedy through his *Gesamtkunstwerk*, to restore a demoralized society to its former dignity. The theatre was to regain its role as the scene of 'festivals of mankind' in which the strong, liberated Germanic hero 'shall live out the joys and sufferings of his love' and at the end, in the twilight of the gods, 'shall in his sublime nobility consummate his love in death'.

Thus wrote Wagner from his exile in Zurich in 1850, converting into the language of culture the thoughts of the abortive political uprising of the previous year. But scarcely anyone paid heed to him because his philosophical mentors, like Schelling, Hegel and their pupil Feuerbach — to whom Wagner dedicated his treatise *Das Kunstwerk der Zukunft* (*The Work of Art of the Future*) — had long been regarded as passé. Throughout his life Wagner complained that his works were not read, or, if read, not understood. In Nietzsche he had found a reader who he felt understood him.

Understood him too well, perhaps. For Nietzsche discovered in the heady world of Wagner's revolutionary writings the world of which, in a different context, he had dreamt in his days in Schulpforta — the dream of a culture of stalwart young men led by a fraternity of wise elders, devoting their lives to the ideals of war and beauty, the pure masculine beauty embodied in the shining figure of Apollo. 'The climax of the Apollonian spirit', wrote Wagner, 'is symbolized not by delicate dancing muses but by strength, serenity and beauty, as in the great tragedies of Aeschylus. Such was the ideal fostered by the youth of Sparta when they trained their slim bodies to new heights of strength and grace by dancing and wrestling, or when a boy was lifted up by his paramour and swept away on his horse to fearless adventures in distant lands.'

Such had been the ideal of antiquity before Nietzsche's eyes during his schooldays, and he had returned to it in his inaugural lecture in Basel in 1869, describing it as 'perhaps the supreme expression of the Germanic love affair with the South'. The rosy-hued vision of Greece pursued by German writers from Winckelmann to Platen was assiduously cultivated by Wagner. His disciple hailed him as Aeschylus reborn, though well aware that the Athenians knew Aeschylus to be a misogynist. Indeed, this idealized Graeco-German culture rested not on that love between man and woman which inspired the art of the doomed Christian culture of the West but on the love between friend and friend, between a youth and his male lover, between disciple and master. This relationship between pupil and teacher had nothing to do with the gentle, feminine values characteristic, in Wagner's and Nietzsche's eyes, of the decadent world of opera and high finance, but was founded on Spartan harshness as embodied in the beautiful but merciless figure of Apollo, ruler of this male world.

The cruel, beautiful youth who was later to make claims for world domination in the form of Nietzsche's Superman stood at the centre of Wagner's society of the future as an image of Sparta. Sparta had raised 'joy in the beauty of the perfect male body' to the level of 'an all-encompassing, all-penetrating homosexual love . . . which reveals itself to us in its pristine purity as the noblest and most dispassionate expression of our human sense of beauty.' It is not the relationship between man and woman, glorified by Wagner in his operas, that leads to the highest peak of culture — it is that other secret love which is so much purer than the society that seeks to brand it as corrupt and unclean. 'Whereas the love between man and woman is by its nature self-centred and hedonistic,' wrote Wagner, 'that between men represents an affection of a far higher order'. In contrast to love between the sexes, he continues, delight in beauty, 'that is, the openly physical, sensual beauty of the male body, is not a self-centred urge but an absolute and unconditional self-surrender in which one feels in oneself the joy felt by one's beloved.' Nietzsche had these words of Wagner's in mind when he wrote to Rohde of the 'double delight' of his visit to Tribschen.

Nietzsche introduces this Wagnerian concept of self-surrender into his *Birth of Tragedy* as the essence of the Dionysian. The sense of bliss that overcomes the disciple in his ecstasy, mounting until 'it causes the subjective to dissolve into complete self-oblivion', marks the starting-point of the divine vision. This state of musico-Dionysian enchantment, as Nietzsche put it, will reveal to the beholder the image of Apollonian beauty and enable the artist to shape his vision of that beauty. In the mystical process of divesting oneself of the ego, the ecstatic spirit senses the emergence of a world of images and parables which gradually coalesce to form the genre of tragedy – always provided that 'the spirit in the act of artistic creation is at one with the supreme Creator of the world'.

The strange anachronism that led Nietzsche to adopt in his book of 1872 Wagner's Young German sexual imagery of 1850 attracted no more attention than did his extravagant biological metaphor in which Dionysus and Apollo 'mated' to form a single deity, 'bringing forth ever more vigorous progeny'.

In the same year that he proclaimed the vision of his New Man, Wagner also launched an attack on its antithesis, namely the false model of evolution embodied for him in the word Jew. Although his *Music and the Jews* had provoked a scandal at the time it was originally published, he reissued it in 1869 with a few even more offensive additions, giving as his reason a hate campaign being waged against him by his enemies. Cosima became infected with similar attacks of paranoia, even fearing, as she recorded in her diary, that the Master might be killed by the Jews, like the Redeemer Himself. The republication of his brochure had caused her considerable misgivings – not, as her biographers assumed, because she disapproved of its contents but from an irrational fear that World Jewry might seek its revenge.

Like Wagner himself, who had been born in the Jewish quarter of Leipzig and seems to have suspected that his stepfather Ludwig Geyer was not only his real father but also a Jew, Cosima too had suffered from this pathological fixation since childhood. Her grandmother, Marie Elisabeth de Flavigny, belonged to the

Frankfurt banking family of the Bethmanns, who, although
Protestants, had friendly relations with Jewish families. This may
have led her daughter Marie to christen her first child by Liszt
Blandine-Rachel. Throughout her life Cosima avoided calling her
sister by her double name, with its allegedly Jewish associations.
Brought up a strict Catholic, she also retained a dislike of her
Protestant German grandmother, who had cold-shouldered her
illegitimate grandchildren.

Similar suspicions surrounded the next in this line of 'wicked
mothers', Princess Carolyne von Sayn-Wittgenstein, successor to
Marie d'Agoult in Liszt's favours, whom Marie described to her
daughter as 'a member of the Jewish race' who spent her time 'in
the corridors of the Vatican'. Cosima was convinced that the
Princess alone was responsible for the rift between Liszt and his
children and also blamed her for having indirectly caused the
death of her brother Daniel. In 1882 she was still to be found
calling her antagonist 'a gruesome product of Jewish Catholicism',
apparently unaware that the Princess's anti-Semitism was as
virulent as her own. With the author's consent the Princess added
racist remarks, in the spirit of Wagner's *Music and the Jews*, to
Liszt's controversial book on the music of the gypsies, as Cosima
herself is alleged to have done with Wagner's late writings.

Cosima, whose life, according to Ernest Newman in his *Life of
Wagner*, was governed by the motto '*Cherchez le Juif*', found in
Wagner a kindred spirit. Very different as individuals, they found
here an issue on which they could make common cause, an issue,
moreover, in which Wagner caught the scent of intrigue. Living in
perpetual fear of a Jewish conspiracy, they conspired on their own
account, and from 1869 Nietzsche joined the plotters. Although
the so-called Jewish question had hardly mattered to him up till
then, after his days in Tribschen he began to adopt a clear line on
the subject.

At the beginning Nietzsche, who had been introduced to the

Master by Sophie Ritschl, Jewish wife of the professor of classics
at Leipzig, confined himself to complaining in his private letters
to Wagner about the 'aggressive behaviour' of the Jews, and to
describing to his schoolfriend Carl von Gersdorff the anti-Wagner
feeling that prevailed in Jewish circles — 'and you know how
widely cast they are'. Then, in February 1870, he felt driven to
make his views public. Under the cover of delivering an address in
the museum in Basel on 'Socrates and Tragedy', he embarked on a
thinly disguised propaganda exercise on behalf of Wagner's views.
'It aroused a torrent of rage,' he reported — not only because it
overstepped the lines of a conventional academic lecture but also
because of its anti-Semitic sentiments, which went beyond the
bounds of propriety.

In his lecture Nietzsche portrayed Socrates, one of the fathers
of the school of logical, rational thought, as the arch-enemy of art
and of its supreme manifestation, Greek tragedy. 'Socratism', he
declared to his astonished audience, 'has bitten off the head of the
music drama of Aeschylus' and thus made itself responsible for the
decay of culture. That state of decay, brought about by Socrates'
instinctive animosity towards art, was arrested only when Richard
Wagner, the New Aeschylus, appeared on the scene, waging a one-
man war against those guilty of bringing about the destruction of
culture. 'Socratism', continued Nietzsche, spokesman for Wagner,
'is the modern Jewish press. I need say no more.'

How this disturbing contribution to classical studies was to
have ended we do not know, since the relevant pages from
Nietzsche's notebooks have been torn out. The text breaks off at
the point where he appeals to his Swiss audience as 'Teutons' to
make their choice between Wagner on one side and the derivative
operatic culture of the Jewish-Socratic tradition on the other. The
couple in Tribschen, who had prudently avoided Nietzsche's
invitation to attend the lecture, were perturbed when they
received the copy that Nietzsche sent them. 'For myself,' an

anxious Wagner replied, 'I can only cry "You are right!" But I am worried about you and sincerely hope you are not going to destroy yourself.'

Nietzsche made a beginner's error of judgment by thus laying his cards on the table. 'Even those dedicated to my ideas', Wagner wrote to him, 'must be afraid of making such confessions.' Socrates may, as a god-like figure, have made certain errors but he is a figure to be revered; therefore he would advise Nietzsche 'to refrain from repeating such views when they are calculated merely to make a superficial impression.' This sharp rebuke was softened by Cosima the following day. Praising the 'directness and boldness' of his approach, since the signs of decay in society can be traced back 'even as far as Goethe', she proceeds to give him a lesson in the art of diplomacy. One cannot attack the Jewish hydra, she tells him, in a direct assault, as Apollo had fought the Python, because the foe, a demon 'emerging from its hiding place in the shadows', would employ all the guile and deceit at his command. Never mention the Jews outright, she went on, but refer to them obliquely, as one does to the Devil. Nietzsche's deliberate intention to cause offence and to disregard people's susceptibilities when it came to 'stating our philosophical position' represented for Cosima a tactical error of the utmost gravity.

'I have one thing to ask you,' she concluded in her letter, 'a request as from mother to son. Do not stir up this hornets' nest. Do you understand what I mean? Do not refer to the Jews by name, especially not *en passant*. Do so later, in Heaven's name, if you choose to take up the bitter struggle, but not from the beginning.' Cosima's choice of words reflects just what she had written in her diary a year earlier when Wagner had told her that *Music and the Jews* had been reprinted: 'In Heaven's name!', she had cried. For although she basically approved of Nietzsche's anti-Semitic outburst — albeit not at that moment and not in that form — the issue for her was not one of differing beliefs or religions but the final apocalyptic struggle between good and evil, a struggle in which the good, represented by the Master and his consort, was entitled to employ any subterfuge in order to resist the forces of evil, i.e. the Jews and their cronies. It was in this context that she did not want the 'hornets' nest' to be unnecessarily disturbed. Moreover she obeyed her own rule, confining herself in her diaries to reporting the Master's own words and letting the veil drop only in letters to members of her inner circle.

The disciple, whose attacks on the Jews, his sister claimed, reflected only Wagner's views, not his own, immediately understood. He removed the incriminating pages of his lecture and purged his writings of all mention of the term 'Jewry'. An earlier jotting had read: 'Destruction of Greek culture by Jewry.' 'Jewry' was now changed to 'Socratic culture', and the rebirth of art — after the destruction of Jewry — was equated with the concept of tragedy. He now concluded that Greek tragedy had been stifled by an 'optimistic Socratic culture' until, 'with the death of the Socratic ideal', it was reborn in Bayreuth — triumphant proof that the days of Socrates were over, together with those of his followers, whether they were aware of the fact or not.

Nietzsche's substitution of the inoffensive 'optimistic Socratic culture' for the inadmissible 'Jewry' sets him in the tradition of Schopenhauer. An avowed anti-Semite, versed in the art of making offensive remarks, like his disciple Wagner, Schopenhauer identified optimism as a basic characteristic of the Jews — a philosophy the very antithesis of the pessimism that he himself preached and which Wagner and Nietzsche also later absorbed from him. Plato too, chronicler of the Socratic dialogues, is branded by Nietzsche an optimist and is 'tainted with marks of Jewishness'. Nietzsche once mentioned to Cosima in Tribschen that Jacob Burckhardt, professor of history in Basel, had told him that there was a great deal in Plato that came from the Jews.

Thoughts expressed openly in Tribschen, and later in

Bayreuth, generally recur in Nietzsche's works in coded form. For
the taboo word that Cosima sometimes replaced with 'Dalmatian'
Nietzsche chose 'oriental' or 'Socratic-Alexandrian' – the latter
taken up by Wagner in his demand that the figure of Jesus of
Nazareth be cleansed of all the 'Alexandrian, Judaic and Roman
impurities that have adhered to it'. On occasion Nietzsche
described the unmentionable race as the 'Phoenicians in the
capital cities' or, in Schopenhauerian mode, as 'that restless, brutal
gang forever chasing after their fortune' – usurers best treated as
the impure 'entrails' of society. After his break with Wagner,
Nietzsche's concealed hatred of the Jews merged effortlessly with
an undisguised hatred of the Christians: the 'total war' that he
declared against them in 1888 was simply a continuation of his
campaign of 1872 against 'Socratic man'.

Likewise, in *The Birth of Tragedy* the 'revival of German
mythology' through Wagner's *Gesamtkunstwerk* depends on the
defeat of the unnamed adversary. Only with the ending of the
state of bondage to which the German spirit has long been
subjected 'by monstrous forces from without' will that joyful spirit
rediscover itself. And to our good fortune enough of 'the powerful,
pure German psyche' has been preserved 'for us to dare to hope
that it will pluck out the alien elements that have been forcibly
implanted in it' – an image of Nietzsche's justification of the use
of force to correct a situation itself the product of force.

Here Nietzsche deliberately invokes the figure of Wagner's
Siegfried, the Teutonic hero who, after years in the grip of the
crafty, covetous dwarf Mime, finally slays him, thereby gaining
the 'treasure' of world domination and, in the same 'joyful
German spirit', winning Brünnhilde as his bride, whose
responsibility had hitherto lain only with the slain heroes in
Valhalla. As early as the revolutionary year of 1848, in his scenario
Die Wibelungen (*The Ghibellines*), the first of the ten-year
sequence of works recreating the Germanic myth of the

Nibelungs, Wagner had made the liberation of Germany dependent on the ultimate destruction of the forces of evil. 'When, O mighty Siegfried,' cried Wagner the prophet, 'wilt thou return to slay the evil dragon that is devouring mankind?'

Nietzsche drew on the same stock of images for the mythology in which he decked the political message of *The Birth of Tragedy*. 'The most painful experience we have had to endure', he wrote in a pontifical tone appropriate to Tribschen, 'has been the long humiliation that the German genius, driven out of hearth and home, has endured under the heel of malicious dwarfs.' But from the depths of the German woods, surrounded by forest murmurings, 'there will emerge a hero, waking from a deep sleep into the fresh dew of morning'; the sound of his horn will ring out, Notung, his sword, will flash in the sunlight, 'and he will slay the dragon, annihilate the treacherous dwarfs and awaken Brünnhilde.' Then, discarding Wagnerian imagery, he adds for the benefit of those in the know: 'You will understand my meaning – as you will ultimately understand my hopes.' Later Nietzsche strenuously denied that these hopes concerned the eradication of the Jews, maintaining in *Ecce Homo* – having now become an enemy of Wagner's, he could no longer be an enemy of the Jews – that he had the Christian priests in mind. That might be true for 1888, the year of *Ecce Homo*. But in 1872 it was not yet time for Christian priests to take their place in Nietzsche's fantasies of destruction.

In the vocabulary of Nietzsche's attacks on the state of contemporary culture the term 'Socratic man' soon gave way to 'cultural Philistine', who need not be a Jew but was 'tainted with Jewishness' and thus the mortal enemy of Germanic rejuvenation. He variously described the situation as 'a morass of exhausted minds', 'a poisonous cloud suffocating all fresh shoots' and 'an arid desert in which the parched German spirit is craving for new life'. Reverting to classical metaphor and to the 'maze that entraps those plagued by doubts and insecurities', he returns to his old question:

'Where is Ariadne's thread in this labyrinth?'

Cosima herself had introduced him to this concept of 'Philistines' caught in a maze of their own, a concept embodied for both her and Wagner in the figure of David Friedrich Strauss, a man into whose jumbled and contorted thoughts they considered it would be rewarding to shine the dazzling light of Wagnerian philosophy. 'We have recently come across Strauss's book on Voltaire,' wrote Cosima to Nietzsche in December 1870. 'It left a very unpleasant impression through its crudity and affectation, the carelessness of its style and the triteness of its ideas.' She concluded: 'We might well turn it into a second dragon.'* This remark is unintelligible to non-initiates until it is pointed out that it contains a hidden reference to an aspect of Wagner's activity of which Ernest Newman wrote: 'There are some things in Wagner's career that it is not a pleasure to dwell upon, and one of these is his resort to anonymity and pseudonymity when he wanted to deal a blow, either at an enemy or a friend, without publicly facing the responsibility for it.'

Wagner adopted this stratagem for the first time in 1836, when he took up arms against the sharp-tongued Berlin critic Ludwig Rellstab in a fiercely polemical article signed 'Wilhelm Drach', which he sent to Schumann for the *Neue Zeitschrift für Musik*. Schumann considered it unprintable. In 1848, under the pseudonym 'W. Freudenfeuer', he attacked various personalities in Parisian musical life in the pages of Lewald's journal *Europa* and, using the name of a Parisian conductor called H. Valentino, took Rossini and his *Stabat Mater* to task in the *Neue Zeitschrift für Musik*. *Music and the Jews* was originally attributed to one 'K. Freigedank', a name which later prompted Nietzsche to call himself 'Friedrich Freigesinnt', while Wagner revived his old *nom*

---

* Translator's note: Dragon = German *Drachen*, which puns on the pseudonym 'Wilhelm Drach' used by Wagner. See below.

de guerre 'Wilhelm Drach' for his mocking review of Devrient's monograph on Mendelssohn in 1872.

Now it was up to Nietzsche to assume the character of 'a second dragon' and to continue Wagner's underhand attacks using a new sobriquet. But Cosima did not realize that their choice of victim was singularly inappropriate. David Friedrich Strauss, a thinker who had acquired notoriety as a radical theologian and author of a demythologizing life of Jesus, played no part in Nietzsche's intellectual world, being considered 'too lightweight'. He did, however, have links with Wagner. He had, for instance, studied under Hegel, a vital influence on Wagner's thought; he was a friend of the aesthetician Friedrich Theodor Vischer, to whom Wagner owed a number of stimulating suggestions for his Nibelung project; and Wagner's dramatic sketch *Jesus von Nazareth* followed in the footsteps of Strauss's *Life of Jesus*, whose most vigorous supporter, in turn, was Wagner's friend Georg Herwegh, who stood high in Cosima's favour. In other words, there was enough common ground between Wagner and Strauss to make Nietzsche's attack on the ailing, sixty-year-old theologian appear inexplicable.

However, during their years in exile in Tribschen Wagner and Cosima had made carping criticisms of Strauss's book on Voltaire – a man they heartily disliked – and considered *The New and the Old Faith*, published two years later, 'terribly shallow'. Nevertheless, as Cosima resentfully noted in her diary, this new book of Strauss's went through five impressions in a very short space of time, something that had never happened to any work of Wagner's.

As Nietzsche did not react to Cosima's punning suggestion about the 'dragon', Wagner himself intervened. In the course of a walk with his young friend in Strasbourg in November 1872, he achieved more 'with a few words of his own', as Nietzsche put it, than Cosima with her anti-Strauss letter, and it was decided that the planned lampoon, on which Nietzsche began work after a few more visits to Tribschen, should be delivered on the Master's sixtieth birthday. 'He could hardly wait,' wrote Nietzsche.

Under the bizarre pseudonym 'Pacific Nile', Nietzsche intended to write a fictitious 'Letter from a Foreigner', a title that enabled him to address Strauss directly in the terms that Wagner had proposed to him during their walk in Strasbourg. 'Someone has told me', he was going to write, 'that you are a Jew, and as such have an imperfect command of the German language.' In the event he abandoned both the pseudonym and the letter form. It was in any case a poisoned arrow taken from Wagner's own quiver. 'The Jews may well master the language of a country in which they have lived from one generation to another,' Wagner had written in *Music and the Jews*, 'but they will always speak it like a foreigner, like a language they have acquired, not been born with.' This denies them the ability 'to express their inner nature fully and independently' in that language and led him to the outré conclusion that 'the Jews are capable only of 'confused and empty imitation . . . never of true poetic language or true works of art'.

From behind their motto '*Cherchez le Juif*' the couple in Tribschen claimed to have identified precisely this quality in the writings of David Friedrich Strauss. (They called him simply David Strauss because it sounded more Jewish.) Wagner's later references to him as a Jewish apologist who did not like Jesus, or as a representative of that detestable optimism which is at the root of the decay of modern culture, show that Nietzsche was made to hound the unhappy Strauss principally because he bore the wrong name.

Nietzsche toed the line. As though working with a copy of *Music and the Jews* at his elbow, he attacked Strauss, the 'cultural Philistine', in imagery drawn from Wagner. The Jews, Wagner had said, settled like teeming maggots on the rotting corpse of German art and caused it to decompose: 'the putrefying flesh is then fed upon by swarms of crawling creatures.' Nietzsche in turn compares Strauss to 'vermin that lives by destroying, devouring what it admires and ingesting what it reveres.' In sum: 'For a worm a corpse is an attractive thought but for every living creature a worm is a terrible prospect.' An unshakable believer in the power of life, Nietzsche can only echo his Master's demand. The supreme goal, Wagner had proclaimed, was 'the destruction of Ahasverus'. 'The culture of the Philistines in Germany', Nietzsche now cries, 'is fit only for extermination.'

Among others fit for extermination was the Jewish storyteller Berthold Auerbach, whose sentimental tale of Black Forest life, *Barfüssele*, had delighted Nietzsche as a schoolboy. Wagner had once been a close friend of Auerbach's in Dresden but now objected to his 'Jewish restlessness' and portrayed him in *Mein Leben* as looking 'common and dirty'. He also took exception to the fact that Auerbach had been married to a succession of well-to-do Jewesses and 'thereby amassed a not inconsiderable fortune'. The reason for this defamation of a one-time friend may well have lain in Auerbach's refusal to take part in the propaganda campaign on behalf of Wagner's operas.

A slave to Wagner's jargon and the ideas behind it, Nietzsche in his turn now took up the attack against this popular writer, to whom he was in reality utterly indifferent. Where the twin influences of Heine and Hegel had once been at work, as in Auerbach – and as in Wagner himself, for that matter, though Nietzsche was probably unaware of the fact – he claimed that he could detect 'an inevitable foreign quality in Auerbach's use of the German language . . . an objectionable jargon in word and phrase . . . false and stilted . . . a soulless concatenation of words governed by an international syntax.' Summarizing his views in a lecture entitled 'On the Future of our Educational Establishments', he called Auerbach an author 'so distasteful that one can no longer bear to read him'.

It was an attack carried out to order. In a check list that Nietzsche entered in his notebook on his return from one of his

visits to Tribschen the name Auerbach occurs under the heading
'Subjects for Attack'. In contrast to Wagner, who enjoyed playing
the role of a sniper, Nietzsche preferred frontal assault. His lecture
on education was planned as the first in an extensive series of so-
called 'Bayreuth Perspectives' aimed at breaking down resistance to
the Wagnerian enterprise. But since such a title made his allegiance
too obvious, he changed it to *'Unzeitgemässe Betrachtungen'*
(*Thoughts out of Season*) − an allusion, identifiable only by those
in the know, to the *Zeitgemässe Betrachtungen* of Wagner's long-
standing friend and supporter Theodor Uhlig.

After the anti-Strauss essay Nietzsche put his list of 'Subjects for
Attack' in his bottom drawer and decided to devote his mind to
activities other than settling Wagner's old scores for him − a move
that provoked Wagner's displeasure. Indeed, a shadow had already
fallen over his new role as publicist for Bayreuth when, a mere six
months after Nietzsche had compared him to 'vermin that lives by
destroying', David Friedrich Strauss died. It was as though he had
fallen victim to Wagner's 'curse of destruction', as Nietzsche had
approvingly called it. 'I very much hope', he wrote in his shock at
the news, 'that I did not add to his suffering during the last weeks
of his life and that he died without knowing about me. But it does
cause me some disquiet.' Years afterwards he admitted having
subjected Strauss's *The New and the Old Faith* to a welter of
ridicule, 'thereby unwittingly causing an old man's death'.

Nietzsche's pangs of conscience were received by Cosima with
disapproval. As the guardian of her Minotaur, she knew that
sacrifices had to be made, and in any case Nietzsche had written
only shortly before Strauss's death that his career as a writer really
had come to an end. So, learning that Nietzsche had subsequently
had scruples about his actions, she coldly impressed on her young
slave 'that she would tolerate no sentimentalities where matters of
the mind are concerned, and if a man appears to have a harmful
influence, it is immaterial whether he is sick and dying.'

7
Bayreuth
Perspectives

Nietzsche had allowed himself to be driven into a corner. The public saw, not Nietzsche the brilliant young professor, but Nietzsche the polemical propagandist for a dubious cause. His *Birth of Tragedy* had spelt the end of his reputation as a serious scholar, while his attack on David Friedrich Strauss had branded him a merciless and prejudiced critic. After reading his 'pubertal pamphlet' on Strauss, Gottfried Keller, a dispassionate observer, wrote that 'in company with a few like-minded zealots in Basel Nietzsche has established his own cult', a cult with unmistakably religious features. The high priest of this cult, wrote Vienna's leading music critic, Eduard Hanslick, 'was undoubtedly the most talented and most highly educated among the defenders of Wagner's cause, but at the same time the one with the most extreme views.' When writing of his 'Messiah', Hanslick continued, 'of whom he regarded any hint of criticism as blasphemy, Nietzsche repeats almost word for word what our religious textbooks say about Jesus Christ.'

The esteem he enjoyed waned in direct proportion to his involvement in the affairs of Bayreuth. So, paradoxically, did his practical value to the Wagners. The more he realized this, and the more painfully obvious the discrepancy became between his cult and the demeaning tasks being imposed on him in its name, the more frequently he took refuge in alleged illnesses and pointless visits to health spas. This in turn annoyed Wagner and Cosima, who attached importance to his always being on hand.

It is a moot question precisely when the peak of Nietzsche's subordination to Wagner – a relationship usually described by literary critics as 'friendship' – was reached and when the onward march of the Bayreuth Festival made him redundant. According to Nietzsche, he himself put an end to their alliance with 'a clean break' after the perversities of Wagner's personality had revealed themselves: throwing his 'jester's cap high in the air', he wrote, he 'danced away in joy'. According to the version from Bayreuth, however, this 'sick creature', for all manner of peculiar reasons associated with his character and the company he kept, brazenly betrayed them, revealing an unbalanced nature he had hitherto managed to keep secret.

Nietzsche could have spared himself much of what befell him after Wagner and Cosima moved from Tribschen to Bayreuth in the spring of 1872. He was far from being the first high priest of the Wagner cult, as he may have imagined himself, to be selected to perform humble duties. At the ceremony to mark the laying of the foundation stone of the Festspielhaus on 22 May, 1872, Wagner's fifty-ninth birthday, two old Wagner warriors met who could have told Nietzsche many a tale. One was Dr Josef Standhartner, senior consultant at the Vienna General Hospital; the other was Peter Cornelius, composer of the opera *The Barber of Bagdad*. Both men had supported Wagner unstintingly in the course of the rehearsals for *Tristan* in Vienna in 1861 and both had been shamelessly abused for their pains. 'Wagner treated his most devoted friends in Vienna like dirt,' said Cornelius.

Dr Standhartner, personal physician to the Empress Elisabeth of Austria and a famous name in the annals of Vienna, not only helped Wagner financially – his demands knew no end – but also provided him with accommodation in his own house. Here, in the course of reading the libretto of *Die Meistersinger* to the company one evening, he went out of his way to give offence to Hanslick. Here, too, he seduced Standhartner's niece, Seraphine Mauro, who had been assigned as his housekeeper – justifying his action to Cornelius, who was himself in love with Seraphine, as the product of his 'compulsive and uninhibited moral nature'. The scandal was hushed up, 'but for all that,' wrote Carl Maria Cornelius in a biography of his father, 'it would have been profoundly wrong if Wagner did misuse the girl in the house which had so generously been put at his disposal.' The letters that passed between Wagner and his 'dear little doll' Seraphine have not survived.

Unlike Standhartner, who stood by the Master in spite of everything, Cornelius had decided to keep his distance. 'Everything has gone black before my eyes,' he whispered to Standhartner when they attended the foundation ceremony of the Festspielhaus. Asked by the alarmed Standhartner what he meant, Cornelius replied, adapting the well-known words from Schiller's drama *Fiesco*: 'All I can see is blackamoors who have served their purpose and are free to leave.* On the same occasion, the musical climax of which was a performance of Beethoven's Ninth Symphony in the Margrave's opera house in Bayreuth, Cornelius and Nietzsche met for the first time. 'I complimented him graciously on his book,' said Cornelius, who had read *The Birth of Tragedy* as a prelude to the Bayreuth celebration, but Nietzsche

---

* Translator's note. 'Der Mohr hat seine Arbeit getan, der Mohr kann gehen', Schiller, *Die Verschwörung des Fiesco*, III, 4.

reacted 'so skittishly' that Cornelius decided to ignore him in future. This unusual epithet was repeated by Cornelius's son when he met Nietzsche a decade later. 'There was something feminine about Nietzsche, in both the good and bad senses of the word,' he wrote — 'something positively skittish'.

In the excitement of the moment Nietzsche forgot to take the opportunity to learn from his predecessor in Wagner's affections certain truths about the Master. Cornelius could have told him a thing or two. Ten years earlier, in a diary compiled for Seraphine Mauro, he had written that 'such was the destructive power of Wagner's genius' that he sometimes considered taking his own life. He also began to have nightmares. On one occasion Wagner descended on him as a vampire that sucked out his life's blood; on another he appeared as Satan, who prevented him from composing and mocked his opera *Der Cid* as 'a stillborn child'; then he cast himself as the Erl King, 'promising to make him his bride so that they could live together as man and wife'. When Cornelius refused this offer, insisting on his independence, Wagner withdrew his goodwill. Initially a victim of shameless exploitation, Cornelius suffered a second time when the Master simply discarded him. Writing about him to Cosima, Wagner said what he said about all his one-time assistants: 'He is one of those I formed in my own image so that I could get something out of him . . . As a person he has no value for me.' To which Cornelius added: 'They dispensed with me because I was not prepared to go down on my knees.'

Cornelius too saw Wagner in terms of a labyrinth from which there was no way out. To stand before this unpredictable demi-god, he wrote, was 'to confront an enigma, a mystery': Wagner's entire life was a complex of 'ethical labyrinths' from which no one who had dealings with him had ever escaped. Moreover between Wagner's hurried flight from his Viennese creditors in March 1864 and his triumphant arrival in Munich six weeks later at the behest of the King of Bavaria, he had been joined by what Cornelius called 'a hostile spirit' – namely the domineering Cosima, who was watching every move. Her new role as consort of the King's friend appealed to her. For Wagner's old friends, on the other hand, she had no time. The pompous style of the letters in which Wagner made Ludwig subservient to his wishes came a poor second to the unctuous flattery and ruthless intrigue of the numerous missives that Cosima herself addressed to the King. Before long she had succeeded in insinuating herself between the Master and his monarch, living in the world of artistic genius on the one hand and participating in the exercise of the royal prerogative on the other.

Peter Cornelius, the petty-bourgeois epigone, was, as the illustrious dame informed him, ill-suited for such a world. From now on the only people whose presence she acknowledged alongside the god at her side were the King, then, a long way behind, the nobility and the intellectual aristocracy. Nietzsche would never have been accepted into the Olympian halls of Tribschen without his professorial title. 'Were there no universities or professorships,' said Wagner, 'no one would pay much heed to him.' And since his reputation as an academic had taken a blow, Nietzsche now had to defend his status against the competition from the aristocrats flocking to Bayreuth by composing ever more fulsome eulogies – provided he still had the will to do so. In fact, his enthusiasm for Bayreuth had been on the decline ever since the Master and his lady had begun their condescending criticism of his work. His style, they complained, was 'clumsy' and 'affected', his philosophical themes abstruse and 'very immature'. His frequent absences from Tribschen were regarded as 'acts of desertion', while his ambitious musical compositions, like those of Cornelius, were seen as a mere waste of time, as though the history of music had come to an end with Richard Wagner. When Nietzsche was made to suffer the greatest humiliation of his life as a composer – the moment when Bülow delivered a withering criticism of his *Manfred-Meditation* as 'the rape of the muse by an incompetent dilettante' – Cosima warmly applauded. In the first place, she told Nietzsche with ill-disguised *Schadenfreude*, he should feel honoured to be the object of 'such blunt truths'; in the second place, Bülow's critique was 'a masterpiece of form and admirable frankness', a further vindication of Bülow's 'reasoned and fully justified brusqueness'. It was also Cosima's clear intention to impress on Nietzsche, who loved to improvise at the keyboard, that she and Wagner shared Bülow's devastating criticism and would be glad if he would keep his hands off the Master's piano in future.

What caused them the greatest irritation, however, was the fact that Nietzsche was a bachelor. They pointed out, with no great tact, that it was appropriate for a man of his age and in his position to be married, unless he wanted to set people's tongues wagging. Wagner had urged such a move on other protégés and assistants, including King Ludwig himself, while drawing a veil over his own marital misfortunes. He regarded his first marriage, to Minna, as the greatest disaster of his life and could barely wait until it was over – a moment that had come with Minna's death in 1866. Nevertheless, he urged all the bachelors in his retinue to take this step, apparently attaching no importance to whether affection, let alone love, was involved.

Cosima was the first to raise the matter with Nietzsche in a reply to one of his letters. 'Does not the lady who has offered you such friendly advice have nubile daughters,' she asked him, 'or is she perhaps a spinster herself?' Like a number of later approaches in the same vein, the question went in one ear and out of the other. Finally Wagner himself entered the fray. 'Never', he told Nietzsche, 'have I sought the kind of male company that you keep in your evenings in Basel'. Apart from the fact that, as his pleas to Cornelius testify, Wagner was never without male company of his own for long, the reference to Nietzsche's 'evenings in Basel' amounted to an insinuation – almost an act of blackmail – against which the victim could not defend himself. 'Marry a rich woman, for Heaven's sake!' was Wagner's parting shot. Once again he revealed how insignificant a role he considered love played in marriage. 'Why does Gersdorff have to be a man!' he complained in annoyance.

Wagner's irritable tone must have made it clear to Nietzsche that he regarded this as no laughing matter. A year later Cosima took up the matter with their common friend Malwida von Meysenbug. 'I spoke a great deal with G[ersdorff] about N[ietzsche]' she wrote. 'If only you could find him a bride!' 'Or what about little Countess P?' she went on, then finally burst out, no longer making any pretence of hiding her profound dislike of Nietzsche the bachelor: 'I find his letters frightening – they put me in mind of Hölderlin.' In a later letter to Malwida, an experienced marriage-broker, Cosima hints that she had only intervened in the matter at Wagner's request and had not taken it all that seriously. 'I have someone in mind,' she told Malwida, 'and the dowry would be satisfactory . . . but what girl would one consign to such a fate?'

Nietzsche, whose Zarathustra was later to proclaim that it was better 'to fall into the clutches of a murderer than to find oneself in the dreams of a sex-crazed woman', was stubbornly uninterested in plans to find him a wife. Since his student days in Leipzig he had loved Erwin Rohde and, by sharing with Rohde the aesthetic delights that Wagner had offered him over recent years, he experienced these delights with a double intensity. On his very first visit to Tribschen with Nietzsche in June 1870, Rohde, a cool, reserved north German from Hamburg, had made a better impression than his somewhat awkward Saxon friend, who was hampered by his extreme short-sightedness. Cosima gave it as her opinion that Rohde 'was a far more significant personality than

Nietzsche'. Writing to Nietzsche after the two friends' visit, she said that Rohde had given the Master 'great pleasure' and that he would like them always to visit Tribschen together in future. This must have reminded Nietzsche of the friendships between the young men of Sparta that Wagner had described in his revolutionary writings.

Wagner too had realized that Rohde meant more to Nietzsche than any 'rich woman'. But his own penchant for extravagant male relationships, with emotional embraces and other extrovert displays which quickly developed into a master–servant situation, forbade at the same time the emergence of any openly erotic expression – and no less among those around him. Like Rohde, who in characteristically stilted language described himself as protected by 'the remarkable impermeability of my outer shell', Wagner would have preferred to see 'Greek-style' love confined to Greece. However passionately he could 'fall in love' with a man like Liszt and burst into tears of joy when he met him, Wagner avoided close physical contact, permitting a more intimate relationship to develop only if there were a woman nearby. Even the sudden passion he had felt for Cosima may well be connected with the appearance of a new Apollo in the form of the eighteen-year-old King Ludwig, who proceeded to woo the older man like a young lover. The former passion for antiquity that had led Wagner to take up the cause of homosexual love as 'the noblest and most selfless expression of the human ideal of beauty' now became, in Nietzsche, 'something disturbing, something that touches on the unpleasant' – evidently because nothing touches on the unpleasant more than the fear of being touched.

So Wagner began to keep his distance from his erstwhile 'friend'. The first serious signs of discord came in April 1873, when Nietzsche read his essay 'Philosophy in the Age of Greek Tragedy' in the rooms that Wagner was temporarily occupying in Bayreuth. The conversation moved from common topics to Wagner's favourite subject, 'What is German?', and to the essay with this title that he had written in 1865, in which he laid the blame for the shameful decline of German culture at the door of the Jews. The only hope of salvation, he claimed, lay in a return to the values of the 'characteristic German psyche'.

While Nietzsche happily continued his lecture on matters Greek, Wagner drew attention to matters German, which he considered far more important. The subject had recently arisen, he told the company, while he was reading the Bible. At one point Luther had rendered the Greek '*βάρβαρος*' as 'non-German' – 'a discovery that gave us great pleasure,' noted Cosima. As the equivalent, for his contemporaries, of the uncouth barbarians so heartily detested by the Greeks, Luther had apparently settled on those bearded invaders whom Wagner regarded as the epitome of everything 'un-German'. In contrast to Wagner himself, who saw in this biblical analogy a confirmation of his own views, Cosima does not appear to have paid any attention to how Rohde and Nietzsche reacted to this invasion of antiquity by the German Middle Ages. But the Master did not forget it. Six years later, long after Nietzsche had become *persona non grata*, he reminded her of the occasion. 'Do you remember the time', he said, 'when I showed Nietzsche and Rohde that verse where Luther translates *βάρβαρος* as "non-German", and that it did not mean anything to them?'

But it was not the two friends' indifference to biblical questions that annoyed Wagner. In his secret diary, published in its entirety only in 1975, there is a heading 'What is German?', under which he describes his difficulties in getting them to follow his meaning. 'If we wish to understand something properly,' he wrote in 1873, 'we must do so in our own language. That is what "German" culture means' – the preservation, in other words, of the received and the familiar. Nietzsche and Rohde, however, appeared not to grasp what he found obvious, and behaved in a manner both

9 Wahnfried, the villa in Bayreuth built for Wagner in 1874 where he
lived until his death in 1883. He and Cosima, who died in 1930, are
buried in the garden.

inexplicable and foreign to him. 'What we shall never be able to
understand about the Greeks, in any language,' he wrote,
reflecting on his conversation with the two latter-day Hellenes, 'is
what fundamentally divides them from us, features such as
homosexual love.' It is a statement that applies neither to Wagner
as man of the world nor Wagner the young revolutionary, but
which seems rather to reflect the uneasiness that had come over
him during the visit of the two friends. That Cosima had little idea
what her husband meant, as she later maintained, may well be
true. On the other hand, she used similar language in a letter to
Malwida von Meysenbug in 1877, referring to characteristics of
Nietzsche's that reminded her of King Ludwig, such as his 'sweet
tooth' and his 'strange timidity', and drawing the conclusion that
it was 'all connected with that matter which we women are unable
to understand'.

There were gaps in Rohde's understanding of the situation as
well. After he had sent Nietzsche a copy of his new book on Greek

culture in July 1876, shortly before the opening of the Bayreuth Festival, Nietzsche complained that it contained too little about pederastic relationships. 'For this', he wrote, 'is the soil on which first grew the idealization of erotic feeling and a purer, more ardent experience of human passion . . . In the best of ages erotic attraction was always pederastic.' In his reply Rohde accepted Nietzsche's point, conceding that he 'should have laid more emphasis on pederasty as the source of a higher order of erotic attraction.'

But it was too late to rescue their relationship. For years Nietzsche had offered his friend his love, preparing him for the renaissance of the glories of Greece in Wagner's Bayreuth by playing and singing from *Meistersinger*, which left Rohde 'wandering in a cloud, stirred to the core by the sounds of this music . . . invisible to the other Achaeans'. According to Nietzsche's prophesy, the cloud would descend on the Grüner Hügel in Bayreuth, where the assembled audience, 'blissfully happy', would receive the blessing of the gods like the Greek heroes in the temple before going into battle against the Persians.

Shortly before the Festival opened, Nietzsche's joy was shattered. In a letter beginning 'Do not be alarmed, dear Friend', Rohde told him that he had become engaged. The news induced in Nietzsche 'a profound love-sickness', as his friend Franz Overbeck described it. He sent a reply the same evening. 'My situation is different,' he wrote, describing such a step as 'not so necessary in my case . . . perhaps because there is something vital missing in me . . . My desires and my affliction are of a different kind − I hardly know how to describe or explain it.'

Instead he put his feelings into a poem called 'The Wanderer'. Striding through the lonely mountain landscape in the night, a man is suddenly spellbound by the song of a bird. He feels a sense of passionate frustration. But it is his mate on the mountain top that the bird is calling, not the wanderer. 'I am charming my

10 Nietzsche (*right*) with his friends Erwin Rohde and
Carl von Gersdorff

lover,' it says cheekily. 'What concern is it of yours?' The only
advice the bird, symbolizing Rohde, has for Nietzsche, the lonely
wanderer, is: 'Go — and may you never find rest!'

After receiving Rohde's letter, Nietzsche, soon to return to the
image of 'the wanderer and his shadow' in a book with this title,
seemed to lose interest in Bayreuth. When his landlord, the

bookseller Giessel, threatened an unreasonable increase in his rent, Nietzsche gave notice and asked Gersdorff whether he could put him up for a week or so. Giessel quickly recanted, assuring him there was no reason to leave: 'the room is unconditionally yours,' he told him. Nietzsche described it to his sister as 'the cheapest accommodation to be had in the town'. When he got back to Bayreuth — the date was 23 July 1876 — he was suffering from severe headaches and his mind was in turmoil. He had already sent Wagner the newly published fourth volume of his *Thoughts Out Of Season*, which bore a title — *Richard Wagner in Bayreuth* — that signalled to the couple in Wahnfried that here was a disciple paying due homage to his lord and master.

It was accepted in the same spirit. 'Friend,' cried Wagner, having leafed through the work soon after receiving it, 'your book is extraordinary!' Cosima, more cautious, thanked him for the 'pleasure and edification' it had given them. If, as he originally planned, Nietzsche had included in his accompanying letter a hint of rocky paths ahead — 'You must be prepared to accept certain things here without flinching' — they would have been on their guard. But, as he feared that he might suffer the same fate in Bayreuth 'as the horseman who rode across Lake Constance',* he decided not to hasten the day of reckoning and left the warning sentence out. Two copies of his book had thus reached Bayreuth before him, without comment and containing only a conventional expression of good wishes, which merely served to sour the atmosphere, at least as far as Cosima was concerned. In her diary she recorded only that Nietzsche had arrived in the town 'as one among many'.

Her frigidity had its reasons. From the day of Nietzsche's arrival there had no longer been any part for him to play in the Bayreuth

---

*Translator's note: The reference is to Gustav Schwab's ballad *Der Ritt über den Bodensee* (*The Ride over Lake Constance*), in which a horseman gallops safely across the frozen lake, only to collapse and die on the other side when he realizes the danger he has been through.

enterprise. The mistress of Wahnfried had resolved to make him a non-person. He suffered. *Richard Wagner in Bayreuth*, the 'Festival oration' with which he had intended to bid the Master farewell, had, as was to be expected, only left him more exposed to the Master's influence, only led him deeper into the labyrinth. Instead of allowing his work, with its dissociation from the Wagnerian cause paradoxically couched in the language of eulogy, to speak for itself, he had decided to put in an appearance in person. Doing so brought him no joy. For one thing, his reunion with Rohde was spoilt by the latter's engagement. At the same time he was haunted by the prospect that Wagner and Cosima had already read his book and drawn the appropriate conclusions. Although he originally intended the opposite, something seemed to have driven him back into Wagner's web.

As though sensing in himself an affinity with the Minotaur, who destroys anyone that falls into his grip, Wagner sometimes behaved on the stage of the Festspielhaus like a man possessed, performing dangerous balancing acts and intimidating his performers by bursting into sudden fits of rage. At a rehearsal of *Siegfried*, according to one report, he ranted and raved like a maniac, stamping his feet and brandishing his fists, then finally seized Siegfried's horn, held it in front of his head like a bull and, to general merriment, charged at Professor Doepler, his unloved costume designer, who had just arrived.

While Wagner played the tyrant in the Festspielhaus, his consort deported herself like a princess in the temple of Wahnfried. An erect, majestic figure in white silk, her hair in a pigtail and with a large fan in her hand, she graciously received the visitors, hundreds each day, who had come to salute 'the miracle of Bayreuth'. 'Usually', said one visitor, 'she affects a somewhat blasé manner', while Wagner's nephew Clemens Brockhaus told his relatives that his aunt had said she no longer had time for him. It was not just a matter of cultivating individual supporters, as at

Tribschen. Now the whole of Germany, indeed the whole of
Europe, was beating a path to their door − even the higher classes
of society, who had once branded Cosima an adulteress, and of
whom she had formerly only been able to dream.

Princes and counts, emperors and kings came to pay their
respects, and she held court in Wahnfried as though she were one
of them. Only after the representatives of ruling dynasties and
aristocratic families had been received, some of whom saw in
Bayreuth a welcome alternative to Baden-Baden as a watering-
place, were the Wagnerians allowed access. Arriving in the town in
droves, they were easily recognizable, according to an English
journalist, by their long hair, their spectacles and their striking
headgear − hats *à la* Wotan and birettas *à la* Holbein, in the style
the Master had made fashionable. They were treated as second-
class citizens, and for them, according to Elisabeth Nietzsche, 'poor
Cosima became an object of intense dislike', as she put on
'ludicrous airs and graces' in the exercise of her 'petticoat rule'.
'Every petty count', she told her brother, after he had left the town,
'was received in audience', in contrast to the rest, who often
queued in vain for hours to be admitted. 'I waited on the little
landing,' Elisabeth went on, 'because the main hall was packed
with visitors. Casting my eye over them, I could see at least forty
kapellmeisters, young musicians and writers, all waiting for an
audience with Wagner. In the end he had to receive them in
groups because the crowds were too big. On the first day alone over
five hundred people left their visiting cards at the house . . . And
everyone spoke in hushed voices, reverentially, devoutly, as though
in church.'

From the hosts' point of view, this was as it should be. After all,
by fulfilling his personal dream of creating the *Ring*, Wagner had
restored to the Germans their long-lost national mythology.
Scornfully as Hanslick, reporting on the Festival, wrote of 'the big
lie of describing this luxury entertainment for rich bankers,

aristocratic ladies and journalists as a national occasion', the majority of those present did see it as heralding what Nietzsche called 'a new dawn', to be followed by political action of the kind presaged in the myth of Siegfried. Audiences in the Festspielhaus could experience the struggle between the shining German hero and the materialistic forces of darkness, in which, in the opera, the hero dies a tragic death. In reality, however, as the propaganda put out by the Wagnerian media made clear, the outcome of this struggle between German and un-German, between the blond-haired progeny of Wotan and the misshapen brutes of the underworld, was far from settled. Even though only those who knew their Wagner, like Nietzsche, saw in this miracle of music theatre more than a crude blueprint for the racial struggle, this was precisely what the majority of visitors to Bayreuth wanted to find. The triumph of Siegfried dominated people's view of the *Ring*, including Hitler, who, following his first visit to Bayreuth in 1923 and with the blessing of the racialist ideologue Houston Stewart Chamberlain, Wagner's son-in-law, set to work on *Mein Kampf*, which also proclaims an apocalyptic resolution of the conflict between irreconcilable opposites.

At the mercy of the sweltering heat of the summer of 1876, Nietzsche saw only part of the *Ring*. Troubled with his eyes and plagued by headaches, he could not watch the rehearsals but could only listen from a darkened room. 'I long to get away from here,' he wrote to his sister: 'the thought of all these long evenings of music fills me with dread.' Still more did he fear the receptions in Wahnfried and, following the unfortunate visit he had paid to the house when he first arrived, he declined all invitations. Perhaps he had the same feeling as Liszt, who once commented bitterly, 'I have no wish to return to Bayreuth — my role as pet poodle is played out.' On a later occasion, Wagner and Cosima found Nietzsche 'so sombre and uncommunicative . . . that over several hours it was impossible to get a word out of him.'

After enduring these conditions for two weeks, Nietzsche left Bayreuth for the peace and quiet of the Bayerischer Wald, making his excuses to Wagner in a cryptic telegram referring to 'fatalistic thoughts'. Originally he did not intend to return for the actual performances, which were due to begin in nine days' time. Staying at the 'Gasthaus zum Ludwigstein' in the village of Klingenbrunn, he wrote of a mood of melancholy that he 'carried around with him like a sickness'. To make matters worse, he was suffering from diarrhoea. He must have realized that, by leaving suddenly in this way, he had put an end to his prospects in Bayreuth once and for all. When one of his students in Basel mentioned his name in a circle of Wagnerians, it was met with an icy silence. Only too painfully did Nietzsche feel the irony behind his sister's words when she wrote to him: 'Wagner is so anxious to have you here. As he says, you always liked his compositions.' As though their relationship had ever rested on 'compositions'.

But the day before the Festival opened, Nietzsche reappeared in Bayreuth. As to why he had suddenly broken off his rest-cure in the Bavarian countryside and returned to the source of his sufferings, he never said a word. 'It was his yearning for Dionysian music that drove him back,' claimed his sister. Less that, perhaps, than his yearning for his Dionysian friend. For that very same day, 12 August, Erwin Rohde arrived in the town, the soul-mate whom Nietzsche had once initiated into the cult of Wagner worship.

Now, however, in the baking heat, surrounded by 'dirt, slovenliness, sweat . . . and other ugly blots on this hallowed landscape', Rohde had only one thought in mind apart from Wagner, namely his little fiancée Valentine, to whom he sent reports about Bayreuth almost every day. 'The town is packed, like a World's Fair,' he wrote two days after his arrival, 'with emperors, other bigwigs and a whole assortment of riffraff', including 'Jewish infiltrators, who can be seen crawling around in swarms'. And Nietzsche? 'Today my poor dear friend was claimed by Frau

Wagner but from tomorrow we shall spend a great deal of time together.'

Rohde was wrong on both counts. Cosima had not the slightest desire to waste her time on the tiresome young publicist, especially as on that very day Kaiser Wilhelm himself was to honour the Festival with his presence. He offered the Master his congratulations during one of the intervals of *Die Walküre,* and Wagner afterwards boasted that never before had a musician received such homage from an emperor and the nobility. Nietzsche's memory of the occasion was somewhat different. 'How typical of the Kaiser,' he wrote: 'at the same time as he applauded, he turned to Count Lehndorf, his adjutant, and exclaimed, "Terrible! Absolutely terrible!"'

Rohde's assumption that Cosima had laid claim to his friend on that day probably rested on an embarrassed remark made by Nietzsche himself. From the moment they set eyes on each other again it must have been obvious to Nietzsche that Rohde no longer lived in the world of homosexual love but was consumed with a passion for his dear little Valentine. It was not Frau Wagner who had kept Nietzsche away from Rohde, but Nietzsche's own annoyance at Rohde's banal preoccupation with his fiancée. He therefore decided to dispense with his friend's company, refusing to see him either the next day or, indeed, ever again. In *Ecce Homo* he scornfully describes Wagner's 'insidious' music as being, through its 'secret sexuality', a force that promotes a society 'in which every man seeks his own gratification'.

Rohde sported over the next few days with friends in the surrounding woods, 'returning from the solitude of nature around four o'clock to join the throng in front of the Festspielhaus, there to abandon myself to the joys of Wagner's miraculous creation', he wrote to Valentine – who could hardly have understood what he was talking about. Nietzsche, meanwhile, stayed in the town, where, Rohde supposed, 'being a famous man, he had to receive a great number of friends and admirers of both sexes'. In fact, as the curtain in the Festspielhaus went up, Nietzsche was alone with his sister in Giessel's drawing room. 'How strange', she said to him, 'that we should be sitting here by ourselves at such a time.' Whereupon Nietzsche, 'with a curious expression on his face', rejoined:'This is the first happy moment I have spent here.'

Rohde, who now met Nietzsche only on social occasions, when the latter sometimes 'improvised very finely at the piano', soon recovered from his loss. His new friend, one of those with whom he had relaxed in the woods before the long evenings of the *Ring*, was Paul Rée, a philosopher long devoted to Nietzsche. Rée had met Rohde through Nietzsche and from now on never left Rohde's side. 'A pleasant, thoughtful man,' Rohde described him to his fiancée, 'whose presence gives me a sense of comfort. What a delight to be surrounded by men of wisdom!'

The arrival of Rée on the scene revived in Rohde's mind an idea that Nietzsche had put forward when their friendship had been at its most intense – the idea of founding 'a colony of wise men'. In 1870 Nietzsche had confided to his friend that he had had a vision of a 'new Greek Academy' to be founded on some idyllic island 'where it is no longer necessary to put plugs in one's ears' – as Odysseus had stopped up the ears of his companions with wax to prevent them hearing the song of the Sirens. The members of this community were to teach and serve each other, using their books 'to attract others into the aesthetic brotherhood', an ideal community of men 'living for each other, working for each other, sharing each other's pleasure' on the 'isles of the blest'.*

To Nietzsche's great disappointment Rohde had rejected the idea of such a sodality of like-minded souls. Yet now, seven years later, with Rée instead of Nietzsche at his side, Rohde himself is found

---

*Translator's note: The subtitle of Johann Jakob Heinse's Romantic novel *Ardinghello* (1787).

yearning for an ideal company of philosophers, living only for one another, 'far from this arid world of the here and now'. Valentine, he assumed, would be able to make her peace with such a situation.

Elisabeth Nietzsche was the first to become aware of the developing friendship between Rohde and Rée. After telling her brother of an astonishing attack on marriage by Rohde – whoever escapes it, he had said, 'should celebrate the occasion, for he will have escaped a dire fate' – she produced an even more interesting item of news. Rohde, she said, had developed a remarkable affection for Rée, a situation that, in her private opinion, was not without its dubious aspects. Rohde had learnt from his future sister-in-law, Elisabeth went on, that, while visiting a girls' boarding school, Rée had caused considerable resentment because – Elisabeth held her breath – 'he had not taken the slightest notice of the girls'.

By the time Nietzsche received this letter from Bayreuth, Paul Rée had already become his new partner. The man with whom Rohde had wanted to establish 'a colony of wise men' had left Bayreuth before the end of the Festival and travelled with Nietzsche back to Basel. He found rooms as close to his new idol as possible, lunched and dined with him, read to him for hours on end and kept his intrusive students at bay. Their days were spent in Nietzsche's darkened room, the shutters closed and the curtains drawn to protect his eyes: two men in the darkness, who had turned their backs on Bayreuth once and for all. Nietzsche gave his mother the glad news at once. 'We are very happy together,' he wrote. Rohde, now a professor in distant Kiel, learnt of the new alliance only a month later. At the same time Nietzsche told him that the two of them were making a trip to Italy. 'The excellent Rée is coming with me to Sorrento,' he announced triumphantly. But lying in wait for him as he emerged from the Bayreuth labyrinth were Cosima, in the role of Ariadne, and, with lowered horns, her god, the Minotaur. They still had an account to settle.

8
'Cherchez le Juif'

The contact with Nietzsche
that had been broken off in Bayreuth was revived by Wagner two
months later with an act of provocation. In a letter from Venice,
neither addressing Nietzsche by name nor signed, he ordered some
silk jackets and two pairs of silk underpants, 'all of the highest
quality'. Taking mischievous delight in provoking a conflict
between his victim's bashfulness on the one hand and his total
submission on the other, Wagner knew perfectly well what the
result would be. Nietzsche leapt to do his bidding, impressing on
him what a pleasure it was to supply his underclothes. Trying
timidly to get his own back, he took the liberty of addressing his
reply to his 'Most gracious friend'. Wagner found this the height of
presumption − which is why it was probably the last letter he was
to receive from Nietzsche.

Wagner's ill-temper, which for the moment he vented on
Nietzsche only with his indecent request for underwear, derived
from Nietzsche's *Richard Wagner in Bayreuth*, which he had
welcomed when it arrived but had left unread. 'Of course,' wrote
DuMoulin Eckart, Cosima's biographer, 'the Master had no time to

read the book but Frau Cosima devoted an evening to it' — after which a sudden iciness descended on their relationship. Only after the excitement of the Festival had passed did Wagner find time to give the book his attention, which he did, according to a note made by Cosima in October 1876, at considerable length. But she was reluctant to record in her diary precisely what had so upset them both.

To this day *Richard Wagner in Bayreuth* is usually seen as a disciple's formal expression of gratitude to his master. Distracted by the incense scattered by Nietzsche, misled by Wagner's over-hasty approval and by Cosima's tactical silence, the critics are virtually united on the matter. Hans Mayer, for instance, saw it as 'a revelation of Wagner's most secret ambitions', while Peter Wapnewski described it as a panegyric, 'an encomium laid round Wagner's shoulders like a coronation robe'. Dieter Borchmeyer called it 'a purely epideictic work', a view confirmed by Martin Gregor-Dellin, who doubted whether 'a comparable tribute had ever been paid to any other artist or philosopher'. Mazzino Montinari, co-editor of Nietzsche's works, went a step further, startling the critical world with the fact, 'largely ignored by writers on Wagner and Nietzsche alike', that *Richard Wagner in Bayreuth* is 'a highly skilful mosaic constructed of quotations from Wagner's own works . . . Wagner is presented and interpreted by Wagner himself'.

Montinari could equally convincingly have demonstrated that all of Nietzsche's early writings are similarly dependent on Wagner, yet, like his predecessors, still have failed to identify their crucial difference from *Richard Wagner in Bayreuth*. For this is not a case of Wagner being presented and glorified by Wagner but of Wagner being unmasked and destroyed by Nietzsche posing as an advocate of the Wagnerian cause. But nowhere, either in his personal jottings or in his anti-Wagner works of 1888, is there a single argument that is not already formulated, or at least adumbrated, in this last of his four *Thoughts Out Of Season*. Numerous bouquets of flowery oratory were delivered at the door of Wahnfried during the Festival: Nietzsche managed to smuggle in a funeral wreath — and no one but the recipients noticed it.

Also overlooked by the outside world was Nietzsche's breach of trust in drawing material for his camouflaged attack from Wagner's autobiography *Mein Leben*, which had been seen by only a few close friends. This confirmed Wagner's reservations at the time that handing over the manuscript to his disciple had been 'an act of excessive confidence' in him. Without betraying this trust, Nietzsche would hardly have been in a position to sketch the unfavourable picture of Wagner's character that was said to have already begun to emerge in his youth — the period covered by the parts of the autobiography that Nietzsche had perused. We light on unanswered questions at every turn, he said — not only questions surrounding Wagner's origins but also his confusing traits of character, 'which cannot but arouse doubts rather than hopes. He was a restless spirit, easily roused, moving hectically from one activity to another, taking a passionate pleasure in situations of almost pathological tension, prone to switch without warning from a mood of peace and serenity to one of agitation and violence.'

'In fact,' Nietzsche goes on, 'Wagner is not a composer at all but an instinctive theatrical talent who, dissatisfied with the easy pickings that lay readily to hand, has forced his way into the other arts.' With something of the dilettante about him as a composer, he put one in mind of Demosthenes — the orator who shouted in order to overcome his stutter — while as a writer he resembled a handicapped warrior 'whose right arm has been cut off and who has to fight only with his left'. Seen in this light, Nietzsche continues, Wagner's career is much like a comedy — 'and a grotesque comedy at that'. Because there are too many forces in him trying to work their way out, they get in each other's way 'and cause him to stumble'.

However, *Richard Wagner in Bayreuth* depicts, not the buffoon whom Nietzsche exposed in *Also sprach Zarathustra* as a scurrilous tightrope walker, but the demon of the labyrinth, prowling along the twists and turns of his serpentine kingdom. 'Deep down', wrote Nietzsche, 'there surges through Wagner a mighty will with a boundless, ruthless craving for power, working its way along paths, through caves and ravines, ever upwards to the light, with the brutality of the horned Minotaur.' Had a 'benevolent spirit' not shown this demonically driven musician the right path, he would never have escaped the fate of total degeneracy. 'Thus can good natures run wild', and even among artists 'who are only pursuing their own moral catharsis' − which can certainly not be said of Wagner − are to be found 'such as have dissipated their strength and become sick, men ravished and destroyed by failure'.

The Wagner whom Nietzsche describes here is a monster who induces 'pity, terror and amazement'. Driven by a 'demonic urge to violence and destruction', he dazzles the world with his own no less demonic power, which enables him, like Alberich the Nibelung, to transform himself at will. Subtly he hypnotizes his victims, drawing them into the destructive web of his own insatiable, power-hungry will, the 'tyrannical omnipotence towards which he is being driven by a sinister compulsion'. Then, in a moment of ominous political prophecy, Nietzsche proceeds to describe the mankind of the future invoked by Wagner, new generations whose characteristics can be seen in the secret runes of his art. The time will come when these generations will shake the world to its core, their arrival accompanied by 'the voice of some mysterious evil spirit hitherto unheard'. And this voice, shrill and frightening, will proclaim that 'even an evil passion is preferable to abandoning oneself to the morality of convention' − a challenge that matched Wagner's own view of life.

But in preparing the way for the generations of the future, Nietzsche goes on, Wagner's mission on earth has come to an end, and he, Nietzsche, is called to take over as herald of the New Mankind. For by submitting to the overwhelming power that issues from Wagner — as Nietzsche himself had done up to that point — 'one shares in this power, deriving strength, as it were, *from* him to use *against* him'. As Zarathustra was to say later, what does not destroy man, makes him stronger. And as in the *Ring* Wotan, his spear shattered by the sword of Siegfried, joyfully surrenders power to his young victor, so now it is up to Wagner to make way for the young hero who is to succeed him. The image of the father who voluntarily abdicates his position occurs time and again in Nietzsche's notes, reaching its climax in *Der Fall Wagner* (1888), where he declares that 'the old god, morally compromised in every aspect, will be redeemed by an immoralist and freethinker'. In order to remove any doubt about the identity of this redeemer, he issues an impish challenge: 'Marvel at this ultimate wisdom! Can you grasp it? I, for my part, shall take care not to grasp it . . .'

Critics, in their turn, have had their own difficulty grasping it. So forthright is the language in which Nietzsche disposes of his one-time overlord that, accustomed to gentler tones on his part, they were at first unwilling to believe it. Towards the end of *Richard Wagner in Bayreuth* Nietzsche goes so far as to draw an analogy between his former idol and the crawling creatures with which Wagner had once compared the Jews, envisaging the Master's end in a peculiarly revolting image. Wagner's attitude towards the preservation of his legacy, he wrote, is like that of an insect which lays its eggs where it knows they will find food, then dies content. In contrast to those readers who were confused by Nietzsche's verbiage, Wagner himself was all too well aware of Nietzsche's real intention, namely to escape from his clutches while laying the blame for the break at his door. When his disciple posed the rhetorical question: 'Could Wagner himself have perhaps been mistaken over this?' the Master was soon on hand to give his answer.

Even without this parting shot – which in any case was to prove premature – the rulers of Bayreuth were in an irritable mood after the Festival. When they arrived for a vacation in Sorrento at the beginning of October, they already knew that the Festival had run up debts of some 150,000 marks (for comparison, the asylum where Nietzsche later stayed in Basel cost 1,600 marks per year). And there was a further source of disappointment. The crowds of aristocracy seemed to have come to Bayreuth less out of enthusiasm for Wagner than from a desire for entertainment, for although they had bestowed medals and decorations on all the participants, not a single dignitary, according to Cosima, had shown any inclination to contribute to the costs of the occasion. Again King Ludwig had to step into the breach. The artistic results too were unsatisfactory, leading Wagner to consider giving up the whole project and retiring from the scene. He even went so far as to wish that the opera house would burn down, while they could then devote their energies to educating the children or join Tristan in his world of nirvana. 'R. is very sad', wrote Cosima in her diary shortly before their departure for Italy, 'and says he wants to die.'

He was also sad because he had to leave behind Judith Gautier, a young Frenchwoman who had brought her perfumes and her charms to Bayreuth during the Festival. She became his more or less official mistress and, in spite of Cosima, he paid regular visits to her house in Bayreuth. 'What joy your embraces brought me!' he cried. And from his holiday home in Italy he wrote to her: 'You were the only ray of love to shine into my life during those unhappy and frustrating days in Bayreuth, and you remain so today.' When the next Festival, devoted to *Parsifal*, was held in 1882, Judith was occasionally to be seen sitting at his side, while Cosima was left to accompany Liszt. (It was an indication of Cosima's dislike of her comely rival, who was seven years her junior, that she made no mention of Judith at this time in her diaries, which are otherwise so frank and effusive. Nietzsche, now also a discredited figure, suffered a similar fate.) Dressed up to the nines, heavy with perfume – 'Papa always with pomade,' said the seven-year-old Siegfried – Wagner eked out a miserable few weeks in the Hotel Vittoria in Sorrento, pining for the new object of his desire. His behaviour had put Cosima in a state of depression in Bayreuth and her condition persisted in Italy. 'Once', she wrote in her diary, 'he dreamt of my execution.' Nevertheless, she was firmly resolved 'to fight this state of melancholy which is threatening to drive me insane'.

One stormy afternoon, 'with the waves beating against the coast', she left her fretful husband and took out a boat, shouting and screaming against the elements to rid herself of her pain. 'But neither wind nor waves heard my lament and the cliffs, unmoved, only shouted back.'

There was a precedent for such an outburst. Back in 1858, love-sick and weary of life, she had set out in a boat on Lake Geneva with Wagner's young friend Karl Ritter, intending to drown herself and seek redemption in the watery depths like Senta in *Der fliegende Holländer*. In despair over her miserable marriage to Bülow, she may have cherished an unhappy love for Ritter or even, as others believe, for Wagner, who was living at the time in his refuge on the Wesendonk estate in Zurich. The scene rapidly turned into farce when it transpired that Ritter too, himself the victim of an over-hasty marriage instigated by Wagner, wanted to jump overboard, perhaps because he was secretly in love with the unhappy Cosima or, no less probably, with Wagner himself. When they got back to the shore, Cosima hurriedly returned to Bülow but also lavished 'extravagant displays of intimate affection' on Wagner, Bülow's idol. Ritter left his wife in order to accompany Wagner to Venice, where they lived for seven months in the Palazzo Giustiniani as *Tristan* took shape. Eighteen years later, on his way from Bayreuth to Sorrento, Wagner, now accompanied by Cosima, paid a nostalgic visit to the scene.

Arriving in Naples at the end of September, Wagner was gripped by thoughts of Empedocles at the sight of Vesuvius. 'The volcano sent columns of fire into the air in the evening,' wrote his friend and benefactor Malwida von Meysenbug, and the Master, 'his nerves somewhat on edge', felt a 'quiet yearning' for death. Malwida had invited Nietzsche to Sorrento − 'a young Greek drawn to the South by his love of beauty,' she described him − together with his new friend Paul Rée and a young student from Basel, one Albert Brenner, who was suffering from tuberculosis and who, Malwida feared, 'intended to follow in the path of Empedocles'. Nietzsche, who had been granted leave from his university post in Basel, wanted to spend the first few weeks alone with Rée before joining Brenner in Geneva. The two therefore stayed for three weeks in a remote health resort in the Valais, a time Rée described as being 'like the honeymoon of our friendship'. As soon as they arrived at the Villa Rubinacci in Sorrento, where the three friends intended to spend the coming months with Malwida, they walked across to the Hotel Vittoria to pay their respects to the Wagners.

As might have been predicted, things went awry from the beginning. Malwida, casting herself as a kind of go-between and with her 'respected and dearly beloved friend Cosima' at her side, anticipated a happy occasion 'when they could relive the joys of the Festival in the company of such splendid men as Nietzsche and Rée'. But, as she quickly realized, her enthusiasm was misplaced. 'Little did I suspect', she wrote, quoting Goethe, 'that "the demons which also wander at night through the labyrinth of the heart"' were already engaged 'on their work of severing and prizing apart'.

Demons and the labyrinth − once again Wagner the Minotaur had succeeded in bringing Nietzsche within range of his clutches. He only needed to wait for him to make a false move. This Nietzsche did by introducing his new friend to them. For Dr Rée, son of a landed aristocrat, wounded in the war of 1870, a subscriber to the Bayreuth patronage fund and a Schopenhauerian who shared Nietzsche's ideals, was Jewish. Cosima recorded with her poison pen: 'Looking at him more closely, we discover that he must be an Israelite.' Noticing that his friend was being given the cold shoulder, Nietzsche became tense and displeased Malwida by adopting 'a forced air of cheerfulness and artlessness which was quite alien to him'.

No friend of compromise, even at the best of times, Wagner refused to meet Rée again. 'He took a violent dislike to him from the beginning,' wrote Elisabeth Nietzsche, 'which went back to his unshakable prejudice against the Jews.' The way Wagner and Cosima 'looked at Rée more closely', as Cosima had put it, must have struck Nietzsche so strongly that he mentioned it to his sister. Successful again with her formula '*Cherchez le Juif*', Cosima simply ignored the offensive Rée from then on, save for informing Countess Mimi von Wolkenstein, one of her inner circle, that they had had a visit from 'Israel in the person of a Dr Rée – very smooth, very calm, on the surface enamoured of Nietzsche and utterly at his mercy but in reality pulling the wool over his eyes – the relationship between Judah and Germania in miniature.' Cosima's allusion picks up an idea in Wagner's essay 'What is German?' where the Jew deprives the German of his birthright by infiltrating the German body politic, not in order to exploit or even control it but completely to absorb it.

Generously prepared to overlook the 'Jewishness' of his henchmen and assistants provided they shared his anti-Semitic creed, Wagner embarked on a campaign against Rée in the clear knowledge that his every blow would also wound the apostate Nietzsche. To start with, he seems to have brought pressure to bear on Malwida von Meysenbug, who wrote that she could not fail to notice that 'certain influences were leaving deep marks on Nietzsche's thoughts and manner of expression' – an observation she could have made equally well about Wagner's influence on him. Wagner then launched his own direct attack, depicting Rée as a characteristic example of the vampire that threatened to suck the life-blood from the German *Volk*. 'He will let you down,' he prophesied to Nietzsche: 'he is up to no good.'

Critics have been much exercised over just what passed between the two men in the course of their conversation. Elisabeth Nietzsche left a highly romanticized account of a 'walk in the evening twilight in a sombre mood of melancholy', an occasion like the lakeside stroll she had colourfully described in Tribschen. But little credence is now given to this, any more than to her claim that Wagner 'suddenly began to talk about *Parsifal* for the first time . . . not, strangely enough, in terms of an artistic project but as a Christian experience.' According to Werner Ross, author of a biography of Nietzsche, 'we can say without fear of contradiction that not a word of this story is true', while Dieter Borchmeyer, in his biography of Wagner, talks of 'a theatrical manipulation of the facts' in order to create what Martin Gregor-Dellin calls the 'hallowed lie' that presents Nietzsche's break with Wagner as a consequence of the latter's belated sentimental conversion to Christianity. Since Elisabeth Nietzsche's account is unfortunately the only source for the episode, many have gone so far as to doubt whether it ever occurred at all.

But it did occur, as Nietzsche's notes prove. Nor is Elisabeth's dramatized account as far from the truth as some, sceptical of her general credibility, have felt moved to believe. It would appear that the conversation – best described as a monologue interspersed with questions – took place on All Souls' Day 1878, a date on which Cosima refers to 'an enjoyable walk' and an evening 'spent in the company of our friends Malwida and Prof. Nietzsche'. Paul Rée, Nietzsche's inseparable companion since Bayreuth, is not mentioned because it had been discovered the previous evening that he was Jewish, and he had therefore not been invited. So what better subject for a private conversation between the two men than this exclusion of an un-German element from the Wagner circle — a move that could not but provoke Nietzsche's further resentment while arousing Wagner's crusading passion? No doubt Wagner would have reminded his stubborn young guest of the beliefs they used to share, of the 'malicious dwarfs' who were plotting the downfall of the German Siegfried, and also of the measures he considered necessary to counter the influence of Jewry.

Ten years later Nietzsche recalled a discussion when Wagner had begun to talk of the blood of the Redeemer, 'confessing to me what bliss he had learnt to find in the sacrament of the Eucharist'. *Parsifal*, contrary to what Elisabeth Nietzsche thought, was not mentioned. Indeed, there was no reason for it to be, for Nietzsche had been aware of the prose poem of Wagner's last opera since Cosima gave a private reading of it in Tribschen, and Wagner only started work on the composition sketch in 1877. In their conversation in Sorrento, by contrast, Wagner's real concern would have been to call his former disciple to account for his brazen transgressions against the dogmas of Bayreuth and to draw his attention once again to the Christian values that he was spurning by consorting with Jews.

Back in 1873, Wagner had urged the free-thinking Malwida to ensure that her godchild was baptized, for only then did one truly belong to Christ, becoming united with him through the sacrament of the Eucharist. 'Baptism and the Eucharist are absolute and irreplaceable; no knowledge can approach the experience of the Last Supper.' It is only the blessed sacraments, he goes on, that can protect us from the threat of Jewish domination, only the Aryan Jesus of Nazareth who can save us from the oriental religion of Jahweh. In 1880 he brought pressure to bear on Hermann Levi, the first conductor of *Parsifal*, to renounce his Jewish faith, not only giving him examples of 'the warmth and simplicity of the Protestant ritual', but also proposing 'to have him baptized and to go with him to Communion'. But

Levi, whose father was a rabbi and who was on occasion to be found allying himself with Wagner's anti-Semitic outbursts, stood his ground.

If, during that walk in Sorrento in 1876, Wagner had set out to convert Nietzsche in the same way, it would not have been out of a naive belief that he could have led Nietzsche, an atheist at least since reading Schopenhauer, back into the arms of the Church. Furthermore, as Nietzsche's notes suggest, Wagner would already be acquainted with the new Enlightenment ideas that, to Cosima's displeasure, Nietzsche had expounded in the Hotel Vittoria. Wagner was far too canny to preach to deaf ears. From the time he read *Richard Wagner in Bayreuth*, at the latest, he was aware of where Nietzsche stood and could therefore devote himself without reserve to the task of punishing the renegade, using the occasion to make it clear to him that any thought of reconciliation with Rée, the Jew, was out of the question.

'Wagner, the last of the romantics, aged and decrepit,' wrote Nietzsche later, in the context of what Wagner had called the 'bliss' he had found in the Eucharist, 'prostrated himself helplessly before the ideals of Christianity, cursing those, like myself' – and presumably also like Rée, with whom Nietzsche later parted in acrimony – 'who retained the will to resist these ideals.' We have nothing more to say to each other, Wagner was telling his lapsed disciple. Nietzsche, feeling betrayed and insecure, understood the message. 'This totally unexpected development', he wrote, 'brought to me in a flash the meaning of the place I had left and of that fear that strikes a man after he has just survived a terrible danger without knowing it.' Not that the danger did not leave its mark. 'As I went on my way alone, I felt I was advancing into a void.'

According to Nietzsche, Wagner and Cosima had intended to spend the whole of November in Sorrento, and Malwida von Meysenbug too wrote in her memoirs: 'The Wagners left at the end of November.' In fact, they had already decided on the 4th to depart for Rome, Cosima explained in her diary for the following day: 'Winter has arrived . . . we intend to leave.' This abrupt departure, however, was due not so much to the weather – a few days later it was warm enough for Nietzsche and Rée to swim in the sea – as to the continued presence of Malwida's two guests, who were excluded from the Wagner circle on their final evening. While Malwida herself was still welcome, Wagner and Cosima brought pressure to bear on her to break with her two protégés. Malwida calmly declined, thereby provoking one of Wagner's familiar fits of rage, in the course of which he expressed his indignation that his old friend should be prepared to sacrifice herself for these two 'whippersnappers' instead of accompanying him to Rome. As a gesture of reconciliation Malwida did at least travel with the family as far as Naples, but had no wish to expose herself a further time to Wagner's tantrums and soon returned to Sorrento to rejoin her two young friends.

'We spent a week with Malwida,' wrote Cosima to Mimi von Wolkenstein, totally ignoring, in her time-honoured way, the existence of the two outcasts. 'We shall part company with her in Naples, since, displaying her legendary hospitality and generosity, which is being systematically and "realistically" abused, she has accepted a mass of commitments in Sorrento in which she is ensnared as in a net.' It was a sentence that carried a double charge. On the one hand, the allegation of sponging is aimed at the Jews; at the same time, the strange use of the word 'realistic' contains a pun on the name of Rée, whose philosophy was mockingly dubbed 'Réealistic' in Wagnerian circles. It was a vicious and unjustified accusation. Nietzsche paid for his own accommodation, and it is hardly conceivable that Rée, brought along as a friend, did not do the same. They took walks with Malwida, read together in the evenings – 'a great deal of Voltaire', according to Malwida – and confined their 'sponging' to the exploitation of her servant Trina, who served the young gentlemen with tea and coffee. When Malwida learnt from Olga, her foster-daughter and a friend of the Wagners, of the rumour that the two 'whippersnappers' were taking advantage of her generosity, she exclaimed: 'That is untrue. They are not.'

Some fifty years later Wagner's son Siegfried threw some light on this episode and on the beginnings of the campaign against Nietzsche and Rée. 'The meeting in Sorrento between Malwida, Nietzsche and my parents', he wrote, 'was, as far as a seven-year-old child could judge, not a happy affair. The fault lay probably with Nietzsche. My father seemed in a bad mood, apparently because of the presence of two of Nietzsche's friends, whom he did not like.' Since the nineteen-year-old Albert Brenner, who died soon afterwards, can hardly have played a role in the proceedings, Wagner's ill-temper must have been due to Rée.

But also to Nietzsche himself. For a year Cosima did not write a word about him in her diary, while building up resentment against him in letters to Malwida and others in the Wagnerian camp. 'Nothing he thinks or says is of much value,' she told Malwida, adding her pleasure that Malwida was 'not disposed to accept his latest proposals' – which could only mean that Malwida should not persist in 'doing everything for everybody'. And although she sent an apparently sympathetic reply to Malwida when the latter defended Rée against Wagner's attacks, she wrote at the same time to Mimi von Wolkenstein: 'Malwida denies that Dr Rée is a bad influence and says she is very devoted to him. But her generous heart is liable to be deceived and I think I am judging the situation correctly. She also begs me not to abandon Nietzsche.' But Malwida is begging in vain, since Cosima has long been convinced that 'in Nietzsche evil has triumphed'. Virtually banishing him from their presence, she proceeds to tell Elisabeth that her brother 'has joined the ranks of a well-armed enemy'. She hopes, she mockingly concludes, 'that his treachery will yield him rich rewards'. Rome had spoken – the matter was closed.

But the war went on. Almost twenty years later Cosima told

the anti-Semitic Prince Ernst zu Hohenlohe-Langenburg that, when they met Nietzsche in Sorrento in 1876, he was already sick and clearly at odds with himself, giving rise to terrible suspicions that were confirmed by his later writings. 'The popular vision of him as the Devil', she added darkly, 'definitely has a basis in fact.' Cosima was given to enigmatic remarks of this kind, especially in her dealings with close friends. Here she is drawing a parallel with Faust's pact with the Devil: Nietzsche, seduced by Mephistopheles in the person of Rée, seals the pact with his blood and at the end of his satanic rebellion against Wagner is consigned to the hell of madness. It was a scenario that matched Wagner's own frightening vision of evil. 'The real hell-fire', he wrote, 'lies in the predominance of the Jews, the living phantom of the decay of humanity', the embodiment of negativism, with the sinister hordes of Nibelungs seeking world domination. 'Only the Aryan hero, incarnation of the Good, can rescue the world from the threat of destruction, and we Germans could be the nation, before all others, chosen to bring this salvation to pass.'

Wagner had taken the solution of the Nietzsche problem into his own hands, treating his one-time disciple from now on as a traitor to his cause. When Nietzsche's new book *Menschliches, Allzumenschliches* (*Human, All Too Human*), dedicated to Voltaire and given the provocative subtitle 'A Book for Free Spirits', was published in 1878, it was put on the index of works banned by Bayreuth, and its author 'formally excommunicated'. Attempts were also being made, Nietzsche told his faithful admirer Köselitz, to lure his old friends away from him – one of 'a number of moves being plotted behind my back'. And indeed, some of his friends and acquaintances, as he wrote to Rée, were behaving towards him 'as though he had knocked over the milk jug'. Even Rohde had the temerity to complain that 'Nietzsche had suddenly turned into Rée', while Paul Heinrich Widemann, a friend of Köselitz's and an early admirer of Nietzsche, claimed that his

11 Nietzsche's friend Paul Rée.

'relationship with Rée, who was opposed to what Bayreuth stood for, cast a shadow over his relationship with Wagner from the beginning and led to its eventual break-up'.

Nor did Wagner mince his words in his conversations with common acquaintances. Describing in a letter to Köselitz the bigotry of the Bayreuth clan, the publisher Ernst Schmeitzner wrote: 'They all stink of incense, and in their attempts to prevent anyone from even breathing the name of Nietzsche, Wagner, in particular, indulged in the crudest of insults which I shall never forget but never reveal to Nietzsche or his friends.' Since he had met Nietzsche and Rée in Leipzig the previous month, it is probably Rée that Schmeitzner had particularly in mind. He also mentions being struck by Nietzsche's 'warmth and affection', while Wagner, by contrast, made a most unpleasant impression, harping on the subject of the Jews and observing: 'There are bugs and there are lice. Well and good — they are there. But we smoke them out. People who don't are dirty pigs!' 'Wagner's followers naturally make a note of such pronouncements,' commented Schmeitzner, 'while some even write them down and use them as dogma in the rituals of the Wagner cult.'

The attack on Rée, the Jew, and his companion Nietzsche set a precedent for Bayreuth. As late as 1924 the *Bayreuther Blätter* was still describing Nietzsche's break with Wagner in racial terms: 'In searching for an explanation of Nietzsche's ill-temper we must recall the influence of the Jews, which had taken complete control of him. Those under whose spell he had fallen had no difficulty, in their turn, in casting aspersions on Wagner's German credentials.' Ten years later Curt von Westernhagen, whose biography of Wagner (translated into English by M. Whittall, Cambridge, 1981) is still widely read, opined that an understanding between Wagner and Nietzsche was impossible because they were separated by blood, and 'blood is thicker than water'. It was blood too that 'drove Nietzsche into the ranks of Jewry in the battle between the Jewish spirit and the German spirit, leading him to launch the attack which slandered, both intellectually and personally, not only Wagner but also all his predecessors in the struggle against Jewry.' The open and repeated use of the word that Cosima had once declared taboo showed that a clandestine, conspiratorial approach to the question was no longer necessary.

In the wake of the violent attacks on *Human, All Too Human* by the Wagner camp came a brief moment of consolation. The letter of May 1878 in which Nietzsche refers to his banishment from Bayreuth mentions an unexpected honour that was paid to him on Voltaire's birthday. An anonymous parcel from Paris arrived at his address in Basel which turned out to contain a bust of Voltaire, with a card reading simply 'L'âme de Voltaire fait ses compliments à Frédéric Nietzsche'. Nietzsche was touched by the anonymous gift. His biographers too have praised the action of what Curt Paul Janz called the 'high-minded donor'. The catalogue of an exhibition, *Nietzsche and Switzerland*, held in 1994 even hails it as representing the pinnacle of the book's fame, and its dedicatory note is still reverentially preserved today. Werner Ross advanced the idea that this 'brief moment of consolation' may have been a gesture from his Bayreuth friend Louise Ott.

The bust may well have come from Bayreuth – not, however, from the chaste and pious Louise, who once confessed to Nietzsche, 'I find my Bible pure, great and beautiful', but from the mocking figure of Wagner, who was once more looking to make a fool of the 'humourless' Nietzsche. Wagner despised Voltaire for his 'anti-Christianity' and Cosima later called him 'the demon of perversity'. Wagner also waxed scornful at the 'shallowness of a mind that rejected Christ but retained Jehovah', thereby allying Voltaire to the cause of the Jews. The day Cosima recorded this remark of Wagner's in her diary was the very day that Nietzsche received the mysterious bust. It was no coincidence. Wagner had long been angered by the dedication of Nietzsche's book to Voltaire and had expressed the opinion, invoking the sinister influence of Rée, 'that the sentiments it arouses must therefore be evil in nature'. On 28 May 1878, three days earlier, Cosima had noted: 'R. had the idea, as a joke, of sending Prof. Nietzsche a telegram of congratulation on Voltaire's birthday.' For 'a variety of reasons' she advised against it. This alone, however, would hardly have been enough to dissuade him, especially as another such opportunity was unlikely to present itself in the near future. What better plan, therefore, than to telegraph his lover Judith Gautier in Paris and ask her to send Nietzsche the bust of Voltaire with a mocking dedication? There would be no need for him to reveal to Judith his ulterior motive.

Richard Wagner in Bayreuth, Nietzsche's Bayreuth obituary of 1876, ironically entitled a 'Festschrift', had caused Wagner great annoyance. *Human, All Too Human*, in which he could find merely 'bits of Rée', incensed him further. Here Nietzsche portrays Wagner as a genius whose mind is so dominated by 'the scent of sacrifice . . . that he was beginning to see himself as a superhuman force', capable of 'redeeming his disciples by his mere presence' and 'quivering with rage' if anyone ventured to compare him with others. Cosima is portrayed as 'the willing victim' of her megalomaniac husband, prepared to divert all unpleasant experiences away from him 'like a lightning conductor'. Later, Nietzsche was to add that she was guilty of the 'idolatrous worship' of this 'insanely conceited, sensual creature', granting all his desires 'from the highest to the lowest'.

Nietzsche must have known that the price of this open attack on Cosima, whom he had spared in his *Richard Wagner in Bayreuth*, would be her undying hatred. 'Where hate is concerned,' he observed, 'women are more dangerous than men', because, once roused, their antagonism knows no bounds, 'and because they are skilled in discovering sensitive spots and twisting the knife in the wound, an act in which they are greatly aided by the acuity of their intelligence.'

Later, Nietzsche was to conjure up the image of the labyrinth to symbolize the danger that Cosima represented. He knew that he had been in the grip of an obsession and that every step that seemed to promise a path to freedom only led him deeper into the gloom – and directly on to the horns of the Minotaur. He had achieved a spectacular escape from the monster's clutches and thrown down the gauntlet to Bayreuth. But the danger had not passed. And if it were to return, as it soon did, he wondered whether he might not after all be able to call to Ariadne for help, hoping she might see in him the younger, and therefore ultimately stronger, of the protagonists. In one of what he called in *Götzendämmerung* his 'famous conversations on Naxos' – parodic sketches of discussions with Cosima, left unpublished at his death – he holds forth on a subject that must have struck terror into her, namely the supremacy of the physical over the spiritual, the former not only using the latter as a mere instrument of its purpose but also providing a convincing explanation of all the mysteries confronting mankind. Neither the secrets of religion nor the philosophy of Schopenhauer's *Die Welt als Wille und Vorstellung*, he now claims, can explain the true motives for human actions but solely the physical principle of the body. To Cosima this was sheer heresy, a sickness Nietzsche could have caught only from Rée, the Jew, or Voltaire, the anti-Christian. The conversation itself, therefore, assuming Nietzsche did not invent it, would have taken place in the Hotel Vittoria in Sorrento.

So we can imagine Nietzsche, the Dionysian philosopher, seemingly unaware of his dangerous excesses, abandoning himself like a loquacious preacher to the power of his inflammatory message, surrounded by palm trees, gazing through the crimson velvet curtains at the plume above the crater of distant Vesuvius, advancing one argument after another in favour of the physical and deriding the vagaries of the religious – until Ariadne could bear it no longer. 'Stop, Sir!' she cried. 'No more of this foul German!' 'Just German,' I rejoined with a smile '– leave out the "foul", I pray, dear Goddess! You underestimate how hard it is to utter fine thoughts in German!' 'Fine thoughts!' she exclaimed, appalled. 'What you spoke was the merest positivism! A worthless hotchpotch of ideas dug up from a thousand different sources! Total rubbish! Where is it all supposed to lead?'

Only at this point did Nietzsche seem to realize that he could no longer count on the help of this Ariadne. She had become his enemy. Her thread, which at another time and under more favourable circumstances might have symbolized the principle of the body, was no longer available to him. For while she was discharging her rhetorical broadside at him, he noticed that she 'was playing impatiently with the famous thread that once upon a time had led her Theseus through the labyrinth'. And she was playing with it because, at least as far as her philosophical companion was concerned, she had no intention of using it again. The thread that had once joined them, he now realized, had snapped.

In *Beyond Good and Evil*, where he carries further his interpretation of the world in terms of the 'principle of the body', Nietzsche gives an account of his life in the labyrinth after losing the thread and fearing he was 'sinking into the void'. 'It is given to few', he wrote, 'to be independent. It is the privilege of the strong. And the man who seeks to be independent proves that he is probably not just strong but foolhardy to the point of madness. He enters a labyrinth, multiplying the dangers a thousandfold, not the least of which is that there is no one to witness where or how he loses his way, no one to watch him, lonely and deserted, being finally torn to pieces, limb from limb by some "Minotaur of the Conscience".'

9

A Mortal Insult

A man who entered Wagner's labyrinth was in constant danger of perishing there − not physically, necessarily, but in terms of self-esteem, integrity and reputation. And scarcely anyone emerged from the experience unscathed. His brother Albert accused him of acknowledging people's existence only as long as they were of use to him: as soon as their usefulness came to an end, they ceased to exist. Even long after the event many such redundant helpers were made to suffer his contempt and his vindictiveness. There was Hans von Bülow, whom he advised to remove himself from the scene; or Peter Cornelius, who had simply outlived his function; or Karl Ritter and Karl Tausig, whom Wagner callously described as having been 'destroyed' by his essay on the Jews; or the conductor Hermann Levi, whom he told that 'he had to learn − being a Jew − how to die'.

Nietzsche too, whom Ariadne alias Cosima had enticed into the labyrinth but not helped to escape from it, found his self-esteem, his integrity and his reputation seriously, even mortally wounded by this Minotaur. He even considered suicide, since for the poison that was gradually spreading over his body there was no known antidote save death — his own or that of the poisoner. Bülow had considered challenging Wagner to a duel for stealing his wife; Nietzsche pondered the same course of action but soon recognized, like Bülow before him, that considerations of age and respect made it impossible. So, not wanting to place himself at a disadvantage, he nursed his festering wound until Wagner was dead.

When Malwida von Meysenbug brought him the news of Wagner's death, she begged him 'to think of the great man in a spirit of reconciliation'. Nietzsche rejoined by revealing to her what stood between him and his former Master. 'Wagner', he wrote to her, 'mortally offended me by crawling his way back to Christianity and the Church', an act that he took as 'a personal affront'. This must have come as a surprise to Malwida, who had known Nietzsche for a long while and shared his dislike of Wagner's eccentric religiosity. For by claiming to be 'mortally offended', Nietzsche was conjuring up the image of a personal feud ending in bloodshed, whereas, hitherto as far as he and Malwida were concerned, both of them convinced atheists, Wagner's sentimental talk of the Eucharist had evoked nothing more than ridicule. Over ten years earlier, for instance, Malwida had poked fun at Cosima's 'exaggerated attachment to the symbols and formalities of Christianity'. It therefore came as a shock to her to hear Nietzsche say that, if Wagner had lived longer, he would have covered him in wounds from his 'piercing arrows' — for Wagner was 'the kind of man one could kill with words'.

Malwida must have wondered where such hatred came from. To be sure, the 'mortal insult' was a reality, and Nietzsche too may have been 'the kind of man one could kill with words'. But his justification to Malwida was flimsy and, since he knew full well that she would report everything back to Wahnfried, his answers were guarded and calculated. Maybe the 'mortal insult' had less to do with Wagner's withdrawal into Christianity than with that aspect of Christianity that Nietzsche detested the most – its repression of sexuality. In *Beyond Good and Evil*, referring specifically to the Greek manifestation of love, he wrote: 'Christianity gave Eros poison to drink. Eros did not die of the potion but became degenerate, became sin.' Maybe the reference to Christianity in his letter to Malwida was aimed at that bias that he later denounced in his *Anti-Christ* as 'a demonization of nature', declaring: 'Contempt for sexual life is the cardinal sin against the Holy Spirit of Life.'

In fact, Nietzsche's sense of insult had nothing to do with Wagner's belated conversion, as he makes clear in a letter to his friend Professor Franz Overbeck in Basel, a theologian apparently interested in Nietzsche's objections to Wagner's religious attitudes. But the time for such matters had passed. 'He has made me the object of a mortal insult,' wrote Nietzsche, 'and matters might have come to a terrible pass if he had lived longer.' Maybe there would have been a duel after all, for harsh criticisms of Wagner's views continued to be heard after his death – and Nietzsche was no laggard in this respect. A few months later he partially lifted the veil in a letter from Sils-Maria to Overbeck's wife, in which he refers to 'examples of base vindictiveness on the part of the late great composer R.W. which have come to my attention' – matters that, however, he said in the draft of a letter to Overbeck, he had no wish to go into. 'Perhaps the most terrible event of this winter – for reasons of which I cannot speak – has been the death of W.' In the letter he actually sent this sentence has been deleted. But he will hardly have been referring to Wagner's return to the bosom of the Church.

Had Overbeck been concerned to find the explanation of this strange episode, he would have needed to look no further than *Human, All Too Human*. Here, in the final paragraph of the section 'Der Mensch im Verkehr' ('Man in Society'), under the heading 'Of Friends', a 'mortal insult' is to be found. Friends, says

Nietzsche, must know above all how to be silent, 'for human relationships are almost invariably based on a handful of things that are never spoken, never uttered.' Thereupon he puts the question to his readers, among whom he knows will be the Wagners: 'Is there any man who would not be mortally wounded if he were to discover what fundamental truths his closest friends knew about him?'

Some time later Nietzsche discovered what the Wagners knew about him and what they were no longer willing to keep silent about, once all links between them had been broken. He had never tried to conceal from them his love for Rohde. 'How heavy a burden it is to be parted from you', he wrote to him in 1871, 'is something our friends in Tribschen feel more deeply than anyone' – friends he had assured that his cult of Wagner always included 'his faithful comrade-in-arms'. While he was staying in Strasbourg with Wagner and Cosima in 1872, he wrote to him: 'We talk so often about you that you actually seem to be here, and it has become a matter of course with us to discuss you quite frankly.'

At the beginning, Wagner and Cosima accepted this situation. But then they began to urge Nietzsche to get married, warning him against spending evenings in the company of young men and finally, as whispered by Carl Friedrich Glasenapp, author of an official biography of Wagner, 'anxiously and worriedly' coming to the conclusion that there was something 'unnatural' about him, together with 'a number of strange and disturbing characteristics'. Then, after the Festival was over, Paul Rée arrived, a Jew and apparently also given to homosexual attachments. This was the last straw. Wagner, accompanied by his family, left for Italy, plotting the earliest possible opportunity, as Cosima put it in another connection, 'to get his revenge by spreading a few calculated indiscretions'.

What Nietzsche had concealed from Malwida von Meysenbug and the Overbecks, he confided to his open-hearted friend Köselitz with remarkable frankness. On 21 April 1883, two months after Wagner's death, he confessed in a letter what was tormenting him, insisting that Köselitz burn the letter after reading it. First he complains about his mother, who said he would 'disgrace his father's grave'; then he turns to his sister, who has threatened to go into a convent because of his 'depravity'; Cosima, his one-time friend, 'now speaks of me as a spy who worms his way into others' confidence'. And finally, as to the late Master himself, 'he is full of evil thoughts. What do you say of a man who has written letters, even to my doctors, to express his conviction that the change in the direction of my thoughts is the consequence of unnatural proclivities – specifically pederasty?' (Nietzsche uses the word in the usual nineteenth-century sense of love between one man and another, as in Greek antiquity.)

Köselitz, who was far from being a blind worshipper of Nietzsche, must have been shaken to the core. Quite apart from the truth or otherwise of the information, the accusation amounted to a mortal insult. Unless the victim wanted to spend the rest of his life in jail, his only course was to commit suicide – or engage in a duel. The operative word, in either case, was 'mortal'. This would explain why Nietzsche fobbed off Malwida with his harmless talk about Christianity, and also why he confined himself to vague hints in his letters to the Overbecks, wanting to protect his close friends from the knowledge of the challenge to his honour that the future might still hold. Only the faithful Köselitz was to be given the whole picture, before he burnt the letter.

But the letter survived. So have others. In 1956 a firm in Zurich published for the first time the correspondence between Wagner and Otto Eiser, Nietzsche's doctor. The editor was Curt von Westernhagen, the very man who had included Nietzsche in 'the ranks of the Jews', using the language of the Nazis in order to demolish his reputation. Rumours had been circulating in the course of the Bayreuth Festival of 1882 about Nietzsche's deviant tendencies and a number of

Wagner's biographers have referred darkly to an incriminating letter to Dr Eiser which had been suppressed because of its intimate nature.

There is also evidence of such a rumour in Elisabeth Nietzsche's archive of material about her brother. In 1931 the writer Josef Hofmiller remembered having heard from Fritz Kögel, first editor of Nietzsche's sketches and fragments, that 'in a letter Wagner had hinted to Dr Eiser that Nietzsche's chronic headaches were caused by certain sexual practices – a suggestion that provoked a furious reaction on Nietzsche's part.' How Nietzsche had come to learn of this letter Hofmiller does not say. But making indiscretions public knowledge was a standard tactic of the Wagner clan in their battles with their enemies. After Eiser's death his widow returned the letter to Cosima – apparently not merely for safe-keeping. Maybe this was the occasion on which Cosima learnt of Nietzsche's 'furious reaction'; alternatively she may have heard of it earlier from Malwida, who may have been alerted by Nietzsche's own cryptic remarks. In 1891, according to Köselitz, Cosima in turn sent Kögel with a letter of introduction to Elisabeth Förster-Nietzsche, having presumably first enlightened him on the 'sexual practices' in question, as she later attempted to do with other Nietzscheans.

The sequence of scandalous events that led a doctor to pass on details of his diagnosis to a third party without his patient's knowledge, and to allow a garrulous quack to interfere with his treatment, is recorded in Cosima's diary. On 13 October 1877, a year after the ill-starred encounter in Sorrento, a packet from 'Friend Nietzsche' was delivered to Wahnfried containing an 'attractive manuscript from one Dr Eiser of Frankfurt on Wagner's *Ring*'. Nietzsche enclosed a covering letter, his first to Wagner for ten months, but did not disclose that Dr Eiser was the physician who had given him a thorough examination two weeks earlier. He did, however, reveal that three 'excellent doctors' had identified 'two sources of infection' in his eyes as the cause of his pain, with the prospect that he would eventually go blind.

12 Dr Otto Eiser, Nietzsche's personal physician.

Dr Eiser had written to his patient on 6 October to tell him of this depressing diagnosis, warning him to rigorously avoid all so-called 'toughening-up cures' such as he had had to endure as a schoolboy and in particular any of the hydrotherapeutic experiments then much in fashion. Although in his letter to Wahnfried Nietzsche had provided a good deal of information about his malady, Wagner was not satisfied. Summoning his assistant Hans von Wolzogen, who had arrived in Bayreuth a few days earlier to take Nietzsche's place, he instructed him to ascertain from Eiser the state of Nietzsche's health. Without showing any surprise that the communication from Bayreuth made no mention of the subject that really concerned him, i.e. his essay on the *Ring*, Eiser immediately replied to the improper inquiry, confirming what Wagner had already heard from Nietzsche himself and adding a postscript aimed at forestalling any reservations that might be expressed over his conduct. 'The extremely detailed nature of my report', wrote Eiser, 'may be excused on the grounds of the sympathetic interest that Wagner takes in my courageous patient, as well as of the affection in which I myself hold him, which has led me to speak all too freely in the presence of the friends of our friend.'

The 'friends of our friend' prepared to attack on two fronts. On 22 October, reverting to the convivial tone of earlier years, Cosima thanked Nietzsche warmly for Dr Eiser's essay, which she had read with great interest, but breathed not a word about either Nietzsche's sickness or the dealings between Eiser and Wahnfried. While Cosima composed her diversionary letter, Wagner drafted a letter of his own to the garrulous physician. After a 'bad night, plagued with stomach pains', as Cosima records, he sat down at his desk and prepared to speculate on Nietzsche's ailments. She also refers to a pun that he made, to the effect that he would expect Nietzsche to take more notice of Eiser, a 'friendly doctor', than of him, Wagner, a 'doctoring friend' – a merely sarcastic remark, since in his desperate search for a remedy for his condition Nietzsche would surely have paid no less heed to Wagner's suggestions than to Eiser's.

A few days later Wagner confided to Cosima what was really in his mind. He was impressed by the idea, he told her, that influences from the outside world might be brought to bear on people of a certain disposition, 'who, good by nature, have not the strength to withstand these influences and become bad, even perverse, in an alarming manner.' He had a particular perversion in mind. 'I have been thinking for some time, in connection with

N.'s malady,' he wrote to Dr Eiser, 'of similar cases I have observed among talented young intellectuals.' And the more closely he studied the manifestations of Nietzsche's character and temperament, he went on, the greater these similarities became. Furthermore: 'I watched these young men go to rack and ruin, and realized only too painfully that such symptoms were the result of masturbation.' In order to save Nietzsche from such a fate Wagner recommended to Eiser precisely what the doctor had urged him to avoid, namely hydrotherapy. For good measure, he quoted a doctor in Sorrento whose advice to Nietzsche was said to have been 'first and foremost' to get married.

This crude interference by Wagner in Nietzsche's affairs has been welcomed by writers on Nietzsche and Wagner with a rare display of unanimity. In his biography of Nietzsche, Janz maintained that Wagner's 'discreet contact with Dr Eiser' sprang from 'a deep concern for Nietzsche's future', while Gregor-Dellin saw it as the action of a man 'genuinely worried about his friend's health'. It did not occur to anyone to raise the question of what exactly Wagner meant by the 'manifestations of Nietzsche's character and temperament' that led him to conclude so unhesitatingly that Nietzsche was an onanist.

But was Wagner really concerned with masturbation and its symptoms? Was he not in reality alluding to that perversion which leads young men to indulge in such depraved sexual practices because they avoid intercourse with women? Why, Wagner is asking, must a healthy young man of thirty-three resort to self-abuse when he could marry and produce children? Why does Nietzsche masturbate? Evidently because women hold no physical attraction for him, while what does physically attract him is subject to severe punishment. Sodomy, to which Wagner was alluding in his letter, was one of those offences that it was a 'mortal insult' to impute to any man – and such insinuations were a safe way of spreading rumours. In contrast to his biographers, Nietzsche knew that by 1877 Wagner had ceased to show any interest in his future. 'Since 1876', he wrote, 'Wagner has regarded me as his arch-enemy.'

In order to lend credence to his 'diagnosis' Wagner quoted in his letter to Dr Eiser − whom he had never met − a number of earlier cases of such depravity. One was a writer who had died in Leipzig a few years earlier, a man of Nietzsche's age who, said Wagner, had gone completely blind. Even Eiser would have had little difficulty in finding out that the man in question was Theodor Apel, a schoolfriend of Wagner's who had helped him financially in his early years. In 1836 Apel was thrown from his horse and suffered brain damage which left him totally blind. In spite of his blindness, Apel continued to make a name for himself as a poet and dramatist, writing, among other works, a comedy that Wagner went to see in Zurich, and displaying none of the symptoms that Wagner claimed to have identified in him. When Wagner visited him on a later occasion, he was surprised to find him 'cheerful and at peace with his condition, which removed once and for all any reason for me to feel sorry for him'. Apel died a quarter of a century after their last meeting, so Wagner's account of his death must have relied heavily on his imagination.

A second case was still alive − 'a remarkably gifted friend of mine', Wagner called him, 'his nerves shattered, living a pitiful existence in Italy, who suffered terrible pain in his eyes at the same age as Apel'. The friend in question was Karl Ritter, the young man who had rowed out on the lake with Cosima many years before, a faithful disciple of Wagner's since the 1840s who was living at the time of Wagner's allegations in Venice. Ritter had published a number of dramas and studies of German literature and, as Wagner was later to find out, actually lived with a woman. Far from eking out a 'pitiful existence', as Wagner alleged, Ritter survived Wagner's character assassination by fourteen years, dying in 1891.

Although the relationship between Wagner and Ritter came to an end in 1859, Ritter's name occurs repeatedly in Cosima's diaries, at times in connection with Nietzsche, whose fate in Wagner's labyrinth bears a marked resemblance to that of Ritter. Wagner clearly recognized this himself, linking their names not only in his malicious letter to Eiser but also in conversations with Cosima. 'I have had some fine friends,' he once said contemptuously: 'think of K. Ritter and Nietzsche.' In the early days of Nietzsche's infatuation with Wagner, back in May 1870, Wagner had guardedly warned him about the fate that had befallen Ritter, without mentioning him by name but leaving little doubt as to whom he had in mind. 'In Montreux,' he told Nietzsche, 'I discovered some remarkable things about a highly gifted young friend of mine.' He said no more, as though he were provoking Nietzsche to ask what he meant, so that he could then describe the dangers into which Nietzsche's cultivation of male company was leading him.

Ritter, the 'young friend' in Montreux, could be compared with Nietzsche in certain respects but not in this. A former pupil of Schumann's, he had accompanied Wagner in his travels through Switzerland after the latter's escape from Dresden, had given him generous financial support and been called upon to perform a number of tasks for the Master, among them the preparation of *Music and the Jews* for publication. When the money dried up, the relationship between them began to suffer. Wagner wrote a vindictive letter to Theodor Uhlig, their common friend from Dresden days, calling Ritter a madman, 'homo pervers' – a conclusion that had come to him, he said, while undergoing hydrotherapy in the Swiss spa of Albisbrunn.

In *Mein Leben* Wagner describes in detail an occasion when Ritter told him of his plan for a drama on Alcibiades, the character at the centre of attention for the handsome young men in Plato's *Symposium*. He also showed Wagner an ornamental dagger, on the blade of which was engraved 'Alci'; an actor friend in Stuttgart, he said, had an identical dagger inscribed 'Biades'. Shocked at what he had been told, Wagner wrote again to Uhlig in May 1852, repeating his allegation in slightly different words. First lamenting Ritter's inability to find the strength 'to involve himself fully in life', he then gives Uhlig the reason: 'He is an onanist! There lies the answer to everything!' At the same time Wagner cannot disguise that his betrayal of Ritter is tinged with regret. 'What hurts and depresses me', he concludes, 'is not that Karl is trying to escape from me but that he is acting like an ignoble coward behind my back'.

Dependent, as he was at this time, on the financial assistance he received from Ritter and his mother, Wagner did not give up. He resolved to cure his young friend's perversions by the same means that he was to recommend twenty years later to Nietzsche. In a letter to Liszt, to whom he had earlier described love between men as 'the noblest and most wonderful of human relationships', Wagner now wrote that he had urged Ritter to get married without further ado — 'otherwise I would not give a fig for his affection'. Ritter obeyed. The result, however, was far from happy. When the matchmaker hastened to Montreux in 1854 to congratulate the newly wedded couple, he quickly saw why. Karl had given to the bond with his wife Emeline his name but not his love.

That love, reserved for what Wagner had suspiciously called 'the evening hours', had already been bestowed on another — one Robert von Hornstein, a young musician and enthusiastic follower of Schopenhauer who became a further source of concern for Wagner. In Hornstein, later described in *Mein Leben* as 'a young booby', Ritter had found 'a counterpart to his "Alcibiadesian" nature' similar to his Stuttgart friend with the dagger, and there was no hope of finding a remedy for the affliction of the 'homo pervers'. If, as George Marek in his biography of Cosima predicates, 'Ritter had hoped that, after two homosexual encounters, marriage would change him', he would soon have to abandon any such hope.

13 Karl Ritter, a young protégé of Wagner whose family gave the
Master financial support over many years.

Even worse – the young men attempted to draw Wagner himself
into their relationship, acting out an 'Alcibiadesian' scene, to his
horror, in which he was cast as Socrates. This could only mean, in
the context of Plato's *Symposium*, that they had set out to seduce

him. Wagner noted in his *Annals*: 'Strange marriage. "Alcibiades" (Myself as Socrates).'

The marriage into which Wagner had pressed Ritter became a growing source of suffering, and he confessed to Cosima in 1858 that it had been a 'dreadful mistake'. There followed the episode between Cosima and Ritter on the lake, then Ritter's divorce from Emeline, after which Ritter began to disentangle himself from Wagner. The majority of the references to him in Cosima's diaries therefore become increasingly critical, culminating in the terrible moment when, as she wrote, Wagner's essay on the Jews 'utterly annihilated him' because he was not racially pure.

It was not the first time that Wagner's insinuations had blackened a man's reputation. In *Mein Leben* he accused the writer and theatrical director Karl von Holtei, who was alleged to have made advances to Minna, Wagner's first wife, of 'courting public interest by a series of dalliances with attractive women in order to divert attention from far more shameful delinquencies.' As though aware of the effect his defamation would have, Wagner went on to add that Holtei's anxiety that a number of highly incriminating matters might yet come to light had forced him to give up his position as director of the theatre in Riga to avoid legal proceedings. Gregor-Dellin pointed out that Holtei's alleged 'delinquencies' did not refer to onanistic practices but to homosexual relationships, and that Wagner's shabby accusations were in any case utterly without foundation.

On the other hand, Wagner's innuendoes aimed at bringing pressure to bear on the homosexual King Ludwig, the man to whom he owed his extravagant life style, have gone unnoticed. His close relationship with the King quickly made him an object of suspicion in Munich. 'Wagner is accused of unspeakable depravity,' wrote Peter Cornelius to his fiancée, fearing that he himself might also be the subject of similar suspicion, since 'people here do not shrink from dragging a far higher friendship through the mire'. As

Ludwig's penchant for young squires and grooms was an open secret in Munich, so too, as Cornelius confirmed, was his 'amorous attachment' to the Master, who surrounded himself with silks and satins in his sumptuous urban villa. If Wagner had had his way, cold baths and marriage would have helped in Ludwig's case as well. But the King called off his engagement to his cousin Sophie in disgust and, as far as the miracles of hydrotherapy were concerned, he wrote in his diary: 'No more useless cold baths – holy water instead.'

Ludwig's irresistible desire for young cavalry officers, which gave way time and again to pangs of conscience and pledges of chastity – 'No more kisses!' he vowed – suited Wagner's purposes perfectly. He set out to increase his influence on the twenty-year-old King and on affairs of state, not only preparing long-winded memoranda on political matters but also indulging in deliberate intrigue. At the beginning of December 1865, a few days before the King banished his beloved Master from Munich because he saw his throne under threat, Cosima had sent him a letter that left him in a state of fright. 'The Master and I', wrote Cosima, 'have just learnt of a slanderous rumour that is being circulated concerning the sacred person of Your Majesty. Our Friend [Wagner] would not describe the rumour to me in detail but he knows where it comes from' – the implication being that there was only one man to whom the panic-stricken King could turn. But the Master himself, Cosima went on, was filled with anxiety and she found herself unable to calm him: 'He does not know what to do – he knows only that he must do something.' She was sobbing when she left him, she ended, and he too had burst into tears.

In order to prevent the King from attributing their shock to Wagner's recent anonymous article in the *Münchener Neueste Nachrichten*, in which he had attacked the Bavarian ministers of state, Cosima assured Ludwig that what Wagner had learnt concerned not Wagner himself 'but solely Your Noble Majesty, and he dares not tell me what it is'. Wagner was, however, well aware, she went on, that danger was lurking, and he wanted to see the 'miserable offender' brought to justice, 'yet he could not bring himself to speak publicly, besides which it is common knowledge that certain people are not above perjuring themselves.' Cosima's sly remarks, made with her husband sitting at her elbow, clearly had the aim of spreading the fear that an unsavoury trial over this taboo subject might have to be held into which the King could find himself drawn.

But the attempt to blackmail Ludwig by delivering him into the hands of Wagner as his only faithful friend misfired. A week later the Master was forced to leave the country.

Did Cosima know what Wagner said he dared not tell her? If she did, her behaviour would have amounted not only to a cruel manipulation of the unhappy Ludwig but to an outright lie. Lying to the King, however, had become a way of life for her. From the beginning she had had to conceal from him her affair with Wagner and pretend that Hans von Bülow was the father of her later children. 'In deceiving the King,' wrote Martin Gregor-Dellin in his biography of Wagner, 'Cosima surrendered all vestige of virtue.'

Wagner and Cosima had early on recognized an affinity between Ludwig II, fairy-tale King of Bavaria, and Friedrich Nietzsche, student from Leipzig. And the closer they looked, the more striking the parallels of temperament and habit began to appear, which led them to draw fateful conclusions, even from similarities in their eyes, considered by Dr Eiser to be the cause of Nietzsche's sufferings. 'Only the King of Bavaria has such eyes,' wrote Cosima to Malwida von Meysenbug.

From the time he escaped from the regimen of Bayreuth and set out on his travels with Rée, Nietzsche was branded in Cosima's diary with the epithet 'perverse'. Wagner had nightmares about him, and his deviant nature was a constant subject of conversation between them. A few days after her letter to Elisabeth Nietzsche banishing her brother from Bayreuth, Cosima quotes from a monologue delivered by the Master on 'the terrors of a certain world' which convention forbids her to name but in which 'no heed is paid to women and the most dreadful matters are discussed'.

Once again we find ourselves in the world of perversity from which a lady such as Cosima can only avert her gaze in horror. Awareness of this world gives even the ideals of classical art 'a sinister, ghostly quality'. 'I told the Master', she wrote, 'that feelings of a perversion undefined but nevertheless sensed had always filled me with a certain melancholy, and that if I had been forced to learn about this perversion, I think I would have been driven to suicide'. This abstruse utterance means the opposite of what it appears to say. For it was not that Cosima herself would have been driven to suicide if Wagner had revealed to her the nature of this 'perversion', but that the perpetrator in question who, provided he shared her sense of virtue, would have to put an end to that perversion by terminating his own life. Wagner saw the matter in the same light. Like Levi, the Jew, and like Bülow, the one-time obstacle in Wagner's path, the ailing Nietzsche had to learn to die. 'Release from the curse that lies on your shoulders,' he had preached to his victims since the time of *Music and the Jews*, 'whether it derive from the wrong blood or the wrong sexuality, can come only with destruction.'

Such a thought also crossed Nietzsche's mind after he became aware of Wagner's 'mortal insult'. Pressed by the importunate Master to confront Nietzsche with the matter, Dr Eiser took the earliest opportunity to acquaint his patient in confidence with the contents of his letter. In fact, he was far less well disposed to Nietzsche than he pretended, describing *Human, All Too Human* in a letter to Cosima as exhibiting 'signs of an incipient mental breakdown'. We may assume that Eiser, who, as founder of the Frankfurt Wagner Society, was clearly biased, informed Nietzsche of Wagner's diagnosis of his condition when they met on 4 April 1878, and he boasted to friends that he was the only one who knew the real reason why Nietzsche parted company with Wagner. 'When, in the privacy of my own house', Eiser claimed, 'and with the most benevolent of intentions, I told Nietzsche about my letter, he began to rant and rave. He was beside himself and I dare not repeat the words he uttered about Wagner.'

After this outburst, humiliated by the doctor who claimed to have 'the most benevolent of intentions', Nietzsche fell silent. He had no alternative, for as the law of denunciation works, by defending himself, a man makes a rod for his own back. Yet if he fails to produce arguments in his defence, he loses everything – his self-respect, his reputation, maybe even his freedom. As was his wont, Nietzsche turned to his pen, recording in a notebook titled after Xenophon's 'Memorabilia', the thoughts that had haunted him since the meeting with Dr Eiser. The name of Wagner occurs time and again, together with Brünnhilde's words from *Siegfried,* 'He who has awakened me has wounded me', which had suddenly taken on a new meaning, and an accusation that, 'while pretending to show compassion, Wagner had hypocritically been spreading slanderous rumours about me behind my back.' Nietzsche also toyed with the idea of suicide. In a grotto on the island of Capri, which he visited in the company of Malwida von Meysenbug after the Wagners had left Sorrento, he talked of 'awaiting the first rays of dawn, then greeting them with contempt and snuffing out his life'.

When he heard of Wagner's death in Venice in February 1883, Nietzsche hurriedly wrote to Köselitz, who was in the city at the time, and asked: 'What did Wagner die of?' Could he have found out that in the final days of his life the Master, suffering with his heart, had frequently had him in his thoughts and even, in an irritable frame of mind, begun to read his latest book, *Die fröhliche Wissenschaft* (*The Gay Science*) – only to 'vent his displeasure upon it', in Cosima's euphemistic words? DuMoulin Eckart goes so far as to suggest that 'Nietzsche's book had been responsible for one of Wagner's last fits'.

And, indeed, Wagner could not get the thought of his one-time disciple out of his head. 'I find the whole man repulsive,' he said, 'a miserable dandy.' The next moment he was to be found railing at 'the folly of the Bayreuth Festival' and of 'building my fine villa in a place with such a foul climate'. There were also the inevitable attacks on the Jews, whom he described as a 'terrible curse', until finally a violent argument with Cosima over a new mistress put an end to it all. A number of things combined to bring about Wagner's fatal heart attack. Nietzsche could claim to have been one of them.

10

Return to the
Underworld

Wagner's death on 13 February 1883 marked the birth of two pseudo-religious cults, both with the same ultimate goal, a goal that soon became part of the nation's intellectual and spiritual consciousness — namely, to rid the world of baseness and evil. In the 'hallowed hour' when Wagner passed away, Nietzsche completed the first part of his gospel, *Thus Spake Zarathustra* — 'the greatest gift mankind has ever received,' as he called it. The gift consisted of a new heroic idol whose coming is proclaimed by the prophet Zarathustra, an idol that in stirring biblical tones and with a discipline worthy of the Spartans would subjugate a world pledged to the concept of the Eternal Recurrence. The dark forces of morality, humanism and 'a life doomed to extinction' having been destroyed, a new age would dawn and the radiant beauty of the Superman shine forth — a naked figure in whom Nietzsche saw the reincarnation of Dionysus. Lord of the Eternal Recurrence, Dionysus was also known to the Greeks as a bisexual deity who appeared as a man in the company of women and as a woman in the company of men, constantly changing personae — the tragic for the comic, the dramatic for the satyric. By virtue of the disease that tortured him throughout his life with head pains and eye infections, Nietzsche, herald of Dionysus, would merge at the end of his earthly existence with the object of his worship and feel transported to a transcendental realm, before finally treading the path that led to a dark cell in a mental asylum and to his installation, decked in prophetic robes, in the arcane recesses of his own museum. Not too many years later the disciples he left behind would be celebrating the miracle of his resurrection – a resurrection not of the body but of his ideas, his words and his works, finally celebrated in the moment when Hitler declared the Nietzsche Archive in Weimar to be a centre for 'the dissemination of the ideology of National Socialism'.

Cosima too was to become the founder of a cult. Instead of following her husband to the grave, as she had vowed, she now chose to set him at the centre of an élitist religious observance over which she herself presided as high priestess and as arbiter on all matters concerning art and racial purity. Shrouded from head to foot in a black veil, she demanded obedience from the members of her sect as Wagner had demanded the submission of his friends. When the French author Romain Rolland, admirer of Wagner and friend of Malwida von Meysenbug's, visited the 'custodian of the Grail' in 1896, he was struck by a number of negative features. 'Unfortunately,' said Rolland, 'she does not behave naturally but is superficial and out to impress, meditating only occasionally on serious matters.' During his visit to Wahnfried, Rolland also met Houston Stewart Chamberlain, who had gained Cosima's favour by describing himself not as a 'Wagnerian' but as a 'Bayreuthian' – a qualification that earned him the appointment of chief propagandist of the Wahnfried circle.

As Nietzsche set out to save the world from the 'slave mentality' of the vulgar masses, so Cosima pledged her vassals to the liberation of Germany from the Jewish threat, from the racially influenced impoverishment of German culture and the egalitarian pressures of democracy. Her remedy for this 'decline of the West' was *Parsifal,* the sacred music drama that embodied Wagner's sanitized view of the Eucharist and the final destruction of that degenerate creature called Jewry. Neither *Der Ring des Nibelungen,* Wagner's life-work, nor *Tristan und Isolde,* Nietzsche's favourite opera, was nominated as his central achievement but rather the mystical drama of bleeding wounds that only a sacred spear can heal, with the Grail Castle of Monsalvat made the counterpart of the Bayreuth Festspielhaus. Wagner's message of redemption, formulated in his so-called 'regeneration essays' of the period following his break with Nietzsche, was directed in the first place to his inner circle of followers, who then disseminated it among the Wagnerian community in exegetic books, articles and lectures. 'If we believe in the existence of such a community,' wrote Cosima, 'it is only natural that we should address it on frequent occasions', even if 'the language we use is intelligible only to the initiates.'

Like Nietzsche with his Dionysus, Cosima had at some moment become one with her god. She avoided mentioning his name, 'cleansed' his autobiography by falsifying or destroying correspondence – 'autos-da-fé', as they were known in the family – and confined his message to the 'Aryan' anti-Semitism of the 'regeneration essays', in which there was no longer room for either his visions of the heroes of antiquity or the humane concerns of his revolutionary essays written in exile. Cosima merged with Wagner as a prophet merges with his god. 'Go out into the world and preach to all people,' she cried to the disciples in 1898, launching the Wagnerian crusade to bring joy to the world, 'a goal even more vital than that of conquering the world.' And in order to 'bring joy to the world' with a theatrical flourish reminiscent of Zarathustra, she had to rule over her kingdom in Bayreuth with a will of iron, as years before she herself had had to submit to the authority of Princess Sayn-Wittgenstein's governess.

The conductor Felix Weingartner, who was at variance with
Cosima over her anti-Semitism and had fallen into disfavour with
her, quoted the 'Four Commandments' at Wahnfried which could
under no circumstances be broken: '1. Whatever is handed down
from Wahnfried is infallible; 2. If you happen to be of a contrary
opinion, you may never express it; 3. Siegfried Wagner is a great
conductor; 4. Whoever does not obey these commandments is to be
mercilessly persecuted, pilloried and silenced, and you are
forbidden to have any dealings with him.' The last was a
punishment that Nietzsche too had suffered.

It was only a question of time before the two cults made
contact with each other. Similar as their message seemed to be –
the supremacy of art over life and the apocalyptic struggle
between *Übermensch* and *Untermensch* – in public they set
themselves up as rival suitors for the favours of the aristocracy and
the rich, of the political and intellectual élite. For Nietzsche,
envious of the magnetic appeal of the Bayreuth Festival because
he had nothing to set against it but an optimistic vision of
enraptured multitudes celebrating the cult of Zarathustra,
Cosima's god was the bogeyman. Since the encounter in Sorrento
Wagner had become for him the epitome of that decadence which
his Superman was committed to fight. According to the rose-tinted
picture painted by Nietzsche, the two men had once loved each
other, sharing their lives in the serenity of Tribschen under a
cloudless sky, in complete and utter trust. Then the frail Master, in
a state of disintegration and decline, had prostrated himself before
the cross, symbol of world-weariness and contempt for earthly
values, leaving his renegade follower to march triumphantly past
him, onwards and upwards, to join the luminous world of his
Apollonian vision. While the ageing Wagner, his heart weak, was
confined to a cold, dismal Wahnfried under petticoat rule, his
young rival was wandering happily through southern climes,
celebrating on the 'islands of the blest' those Dionysian rituals at

which, in the provocative words of Zarathustra, 'the gods shed their clothes in the frenzy of the dance'.

Revenge too formed part of the picture. Nietzsche now attacked his adversary on two fronts. First he insinuated that Wagner was actually Jewish himself, being the natural son — as Nietzsche claimed to have found in Wagner's autobiography — of his stepfather Ludwig Geyer. The name Geyer means 'vulture' and has Jewish associations; while the family name Adler (= 'eagle') is thoroughly Jewish. Warming to his malicious task, Nietzsche plays on the two bird names in *The Case of Wagner*: 'A "Geyer" is all but an "Adler".' With his eye on Wagner's essay *What Is German?* he then poses the extraordinary question 'Was Wagner really German at all?', answering his own question by calling Wagner a Semite and concluding: 'Now we can understand his antipathy towards the Jews.' His admirer Resa von Schirnhofer — a young student to whom he made it clear, when she visited him in Nice in 1884, that he had no inclination to get married — said he once told her that Wagner had Jewish blood in his veins. 'Although Nietzsche had previously never spoken to me in a derogatory way about the Jews,' she wrote, 'he did so on this occasion with at least a hint of derision.'

Nietzsche's second line of attack against 'Wagner the liar' and his bogus cult in Bayreuth was his way of getting his own back for the 'mortal insult' to which Wagner had earlier subjected him. In reality, he now says, Wagner is not a man at all, but is of 'feminine gender', not in the sense of the frailty that comes with advancing years but of a perversion that runs through his entire life. Wagner, he trumpeted for all to hear, was perverse, living 'under the spell of that improbable pathological sexuality that had been the curse of his whole existence'. Writing to Malwida, he said: 'You can have no conception of the disgust with which I turned my back on Wagner ten years ago . . . or of the profundity of the revulsion I have instilled in people against the disgusting sexuality in his music.' For this music, he went on, not without a tinge of hypocrisy, induces in its listeners a state of extreme physical agitation akin to sexual stimulation, 'with panting and irregular breathing, flushes of blood, extreme passion followed by a sudden coma' – in short, an orgasm in music, at the prospect of which Nietzsche, protagonist of sexual libertarianism, appears to be crossing himself in fear. Moreover he found it particularly galling that Wagner, master of ambiguity, should have had his final and perhaps greatest success with *Parsifal*, a work in praise of chastity, an 'inspired masterpiece of seduction' whose true nature an ecstatic Christian community had failed to recognize.

Nietzsche's words may have sprung from envy and a desire for revenge, but they were uncannily perceptive. *Parsifal*, performed in Cosima's Bayreuth like a celebration of high mass in an atmosphere 'redolent partly of a church, partly of a brothel', appeared even to sober-minded audiences like an imperial, neo-Gothic extravaganza. Its sublime choirs of angels and music of the spheres contrasting grotesquely with the stuffed birds and the battery-powered glow of the Grail, it fulfilled the needs of those 'who have long been incapable of distinguishing between self-indulgence and aesthetic pleasure'.

Such was the impression made on Elisabeth von Herzogenberg, wife of the composer Heinrich von Herzogenberg, when she attended the Bayreuth Festival in 1889, the year of Nietzsche's breakdown. She found audiences at *Parsifal* 'in an unnatural state of wild hysteria', with the Festspielhaus 'like a church . . . smothered in a gory ritual and full of the musty scent of incense', while the work itself, 'with its fetid sensuality and its religious posturings', literally took one's breath away – or, as Nietzsche had put it, induced in the faithful a state of 'extreme physical agitation'.

Nietzsche was convinced that the guilt for this collective 'prostration before the cross' lay entirely with Cosima. While conceding that she was the only woman 'of real stature' he had ever met, he accused her of perverting Wagner and making him the centre of an idolatrous cult. In a letter of condolence he sent to her on Wagner's death, he conceded that she had 'lived for one purpose and one alone, and had sacrificed everything to this purpose'. But in the draft of his letter he had originally written that she had 'lived for one urge and one alone, and sacrificed everything to this urge' – namely, first to worship Wagner's 'highest and lowest desires', then to consolidate his entire work into an idolatrous cult. Elsewhere he maintained that no one knew better than Cosima 'how I had penetrated the secret corners of Wagner's mind', hidden areas of which nobody was aware but him – 'not even Frau Cosima. And she knows I am right.'

Cosima was not one to let such remarks go unanswered. In letters to her faithful 'companions of the Grail', she expressed her supreme contempt for Nietzsche and supplied them with ammunition to continue the attack on their own. From childhood, she told them, he had been 'a sickly creature . . . incapable of being happy or cheerful', which had led her children 'to feel genuinely frightened of him'. And although, with his nervelessness, his 'unnatural timidity' and the 'general effeminacy of his ways', he was scarcely to be regarded as a proper man at all, he had nonetheless 'offended the feminine sex by failing to recognize its sublime mission, whatever the ways in which it might pursue that mission.' Nietzsche's works, she went on, were like 'spasms of impotence, full of despicable malice', and consisted of elements cobbled together from all manner of sources: 'Indeed, we could prove where every sentence of Nietzsche's comes from.' He then procedes to offset this 'utter lack of originality' by a display of megalomania – the same phenomenon Wagner had demonstrated in his *Music and the Jews* – which, Cosima concluded, at least had the advantage of revealing through his neurosis 'the truth about his mean and contemptible character'.

As Nietzsche had attacked *Parsifal,* so Cosima now rounded on *Zarathustra.* 'We subjected ourselves to the agony of reading this

work', she wrote in 1901 to Houston Stewart Chamberlain, 'and
were not only amazed at its stupidity but found that it aroused
certain suspicions on linguistic grounds.' 'What Nietzsche writes is
not German,' she continued: 'his jerky sentences, depressingly
monotonous, belong to no language I know — the closest might be
that of the Old Testament.' Cosima sees in this the reason for 'the
most repulsive aspect of Nietzsche', namely, 'that he dragged
Christianity into his distorted conception and replaced the true
God with a bacchanalian deity for which the only possible
inspiration could have been King David prancing before the Ark of
the Covenant.' Thus Cosima claimed to have detected the presence
of 'Jewishness' in Nietzsche's prophecy of the Superman. She
would nevertheless have been prepared, she added, to attribute
these hideous features, together with his 'empty ideas' and 'moral
depravity', to his mental condition, had there not been, to her
considerable anger, 'so much fuss about this lamentable book'.

Cosima would have rather seen this 'fuss' reserved for
Bayreuth. But even without her propaganda machine and the
annual Wagner Festival, her adversary was proving to be an ideal
cult figure for a nation that had visions of world domination. The
faith that sustained the Second Reich embraced not only a
Germanic ideal purged of racial impurities, as preached by
Wagner, but also the vision of a 'will to power', bereft of all
unmanly, effeminate elements, as proclaimed by Nietzsche. In
Weimar, Cosima noted with suspicion, a rival clique was
developing that attracted an ever growing number of disciples and
patrons — 'Nietzscheans' who looked down on the 'decadence' of
Bayreuth with an arrogance characteristic, in Cosima's eyes, of 'the
barbaric perversity of our age'. If only Nietzsche had quietly
resigned himself to his condition, she complained two years after
his death, and met his end calmly and peacefully — 'as many
others have done' — one could have drawn a veil over the whole
episode. Instead, 'a sorry cult' had grown up round his late works,

the most disturbing characteristics of which were 'its obfuscation and its presumptuousness'.

Nietzsche's sister, who had once looked after the Wagner children in Wahnfried and now, acting like a priestess of the philosophy of 'God is dead', brazenly set herself up in Weimar in the role that Cosima played in Bayreuth, became a particular object of Cosima's animosity. Elisabeth, nine years younger than her rival, was driven by the very 'will to power' of which she accused Cosima, and was no less adept at promoting her cause. Turning Nietzsche's sick-room into a place of pilgrimage for his disciples, she conjured out of the chaotic jottings in which he had recorded his flashes of inspiration the book that came to bear the title *Der Wille zur Macht* (*The Will to Power*), an epoch-making work that sought to give his scattered thoughts on subjects such as morality and discipline the status of dogma. Acolytes, meanwhile, continued to issue their encyclicals from Weimar. As an editor, too, Elisabeth proved the equal of her rival in Bayreuth: she lied and forged, destroying material on the one hand and so lovingly distorting it on the other that it seemed as though the author himself had taken control of her. As Cosima felt herself to be the reincarnation of the Master, so those of her own inner circle claimed Elisabeth to be the embodiment of her brother, even if only in the form of a caricature.

Because she had secretly and enviously adopted the Bayreuth cult as her model, Elisabeth was at pains to preserve as harmonious and dignified a relationship with Wahnfried as possible, posing as 'a Cosima Nietzsche', as Josef Hofmiller put it. The mistress of Bayreuth, irritated by Elisabeth's pretentious airs and graces, was not amused. At a social gathering in the house of Meyerbeer's daughter she turned her back on her rival, and Elisabeth's eyes filled with tears. Cosima could not forgive her for courting fame on her own behalf 'by using a poor sick man to make many others sick as well'. For, as Cosima had observed, Nietzsche was infectious, and to have acknowledged his sister in public might well have spread the epidemic still further. When, after Nietzsche's death, Elisabeth claimed to be Cosima's equal, since, as she put it, 'the two philosophical movements that dominate the modern world are now both led by women', Cosima burst out laughing.

And Cosima was about to deal her opponent a second blow. Elisabeth had asked to have the extensive correspondence between her brother and the Wagners made available to her. This, Cosima replied, would unfortunately not be possible, 'because in accordance with the custom, not to say principle, at Wahnfried your brother's letters have been destroyed.' Carl Maria Cornelius met with a similar response when he asked for the letters his father had written to Wagner. No one was interested in publishing these letters, Cosima told him, so, except for the occasional item, everything addressed to Wagner from people like Heine, Berlioz, Georg Herwegh, the Wesendonks, Baudelaire, Bülow, Nietzsche, Gobineau and others had been disposed of.

Where Nietzsche was concerned, Cosima would dearly have loved to destroy his works as well. Since, given the superior role she had assumed, she could hardly afford to embark on a feud herself, she repeatedly goaded her minions into writing articles and letters attacking the demented philosopher and the Weimar cult of the Superman. When Gustav Schönaich, one of her intimates, wrote to her to convey his hostility to Nietzsche, she urged him to develop his ideas into a public lecture, then called on Carl Friedrich Glasenapp, 'court biographer' of Wagner, to deliver an anti-Nietzsche polemic against 'this heartless, revolting creature, filled, as he is, with conceit and pompous stupidity'. She pestered Chamberlain – with whom she carried on a mildly amorous correspondence – to launch an attack on *Zarathustra* by making its author out to be 'either a monster or a madman'. This pandered to an obsession Cosima and Chamberlain had shared for a long time. 'Where Nietzsche is concerned,' she wrote to him, 'I detect something that touches on the deepest problems of metaphysics. Race also has something to do with it — for he was of Slav descent.' As she told Mimi von Wolkenstein with characteristic spitefulness, this could only mean one thing: 'I was amused to learn that, in terms of people you dislike, you include the Slavs with our Israelite brethren.' Nietzsche, in other words, was a kind of Jew after all. The Master's triumph was complete.

Chamberlain hesitated to do her bidding. Noble task that it was to take up arms for his Lady Cosima, 'like a hero eager to slay the dragon of the detested Nietzsche cult', as Massimo Zumbini wrote, Chamberlain, as a pragmatist anxious not to ruin his reputation with the Nietzschean camp, considered it an unwise move. The Zarathustrans, moreover, pursued pan-Germanic nationalistic goals similar to those he had long advocated in his own writings. He was also reluctant to dwell on Nietzsche's personal life, about which he had learnt disturbing things from a common friend — 'confidential information about the "secret" at the heart of Nietzsche's life'. 'This', wrote Chamberlain to his 'honoured lady', 'is why from the very beginning there was no place in my life for Nietzsche. And when one knows that, one can only be repelled by all his prattle about a dominant male nature.' Cosima made no attempt to find out what the secret was.

The two antagonistic cults, which continued their feud with the same violence as their two idols had done, were to achieve a public reconciliation under the auspices of the enthusiastic Wagnero-Nietzschean Adolf Hitler. Elisabeth Förster-Nietzsche's funeral, held with characteristic Nazi pomp in the presence of a tearful Führer in November 1935, was attended — probably in deference to Hitler himself — by Siegfried Wagner's widow Winifred, who had inherited the Bayreuth legacy on Cosima's death in 1930. The year before Elisabeth died, Hitler had planned to build a commemorative Zarathustra monument to Nietzsche that would incorporate a statue of Dionysus donated by Mussolini, also an avid reader of Nietzsche's works. An even grander memorial was proposed for Bayreuth, where a palatial marble acropolis was to be crowned by the regal Festspielhaus as its Parthenon. Here the ultimate victory would be celebrated in *Parsifal.* But preoccupation with the wars that Nietzsche had prophesied would ravage the twentieth century caused Hitler to lose interest in the projects, and the two parties, unable to make common cause, quickly resumed their old feuding ways.

If Nietzsche had his way, there would have been no need for this. For the bitter attacks on Wagner that reached their climax in his furious outbursts of 1888, as though his enemy were still alive, were in reality a continuation of the old war. He had unmasked the decadent, perverse, ignoble aspects of Wagner's work and disposed of them once and for all. As for Wagner's heroic, superhuman achievements, on the other hand – the divine quality that sprang from his Dionysian incarnation – they now found their embodiment in Nietzsche himself. As early as 1882 he had told Malwida von Meysenbug that 'the best of Wagner's achievement' would live on in him. Six years later he described his *Thoughts out of Season* as prophesies of his own future. 'At all vital psychological moments', he said, 'it is I who am the real subject and, wherever the name Wagner occurs, the name Nietzsche can be substituted without reservation.' 'Wagner' was to become one of his most frequently used words in the final year of his creative life.

Wagner's death in 1883 not only reopened the wound of his 'mortal insult' but also marked the re-emergence of a claim that had long seemed dead and buried. 'At the end', wrote Nietzsche to Köselitz a few days after the Master died, 'it was the ageing Wagner against whom I had to defend myself. As far as the real Wagner is concerned, I count on inheriting a large part of his legacy myself.' He even promised that Köselitz's compositions, like the 'shamefully misunderstood' opera *The Lion of Venice*, would be given a position of honour. 'Many things have now become possible,' he exclaimed ecstatically, 'such as to sit in the Bayreuth temple again and listen this time to *your* music.' To set *The Lion of Venice* alongside *Parsifal* was one of Nietzsche's cherished illusions, a parallel to the vision of a 'fraternity of wise men' living on 'the isles of the blest'. In his dreams, the Green Hill in Bayreuth, deprived of its lord and master, became transformed into the desolate shore of Naxos, where, like the deserted Ariadne, the exhausted Cosima has cried herself to sleep in her grief. 'Abandoned by her hero, Ariadne dreams of the Super-hero,' wrote Nietzsche in the summer following Wagner's death. This Super-hero takes the form of 'Dionysus on the Tiger', who first subjects a cruel Nature to his will, then tames the capricious Princess. For he is equally entitled to Ariadne as his bride as, in the role of Wagner's heir, he is to Cosima, Wagner's widow. But Cosima does not yet realize this, so, in the teasing, mischievous manner that reflects his Dionysian nature, Nietzsche has to resort to hints and subtle allusions in his works in order to help her grasp the situation.

In the autumn of 1887, the Super-hero, luxuriating in thoughts on the mysterious relationship between cruelty and the sexual urge, reflected on the destructive power 'that subtly stimulates our pleasure in cruelty' and conceived the concept of the 'thrill of destruction', as embodied in the mythological figure of the Minotaur. A 'sado-masochist', as his friend Lou Salomé described him, he was now in his element − a world to which also belonged, since the Tribschen era, his 'satyr drama' of Dionysus, Ariadne and Theseus, scenes from which, with the figure of Cosima-Ariadne in mind, he had incorporated with mystifying intent (see above p. 72) into several of his books. Now he judged the time to be ripe for a return to that world, adding new scenes and fragments of dialogue, generally of a light-hearted nature, which baffled readers and led even an acute critic like Erich F. Podach to dismiss them as 'empty chatter' and 'fatuous bombast'.

But as he set about his task, relaxed and at ease, Nietzsche knew that there was one person who would understand his 'empty chatter' — she had, after all, been involved in it. For the seemingly meaningless phrases belong to the period of Cosima's divorce, when bitter arguments took place between her, her lover and her cuckolded husband which Bülow repeated to Nietzsche in Basel, often, one imagines, word for word. The episode of her adultery, into which even King Ludwig of Bavaria had been drawn, was the most traumatic experience in her life. Nietzsche had himself witnessed the events in Tribschen and, playing on this weakness in the 'iron lady', he now plunged his dagger into the old wound. By dragging up her transgression, he assumed the role of the agent of 'inexorable justice' that Cosima herself had set out to play in the past. The whole purpose of his satyric drama was to torment her, while also reminding her of her mythological identity. You are Ariadne, he told her, deserted by the hero and in need of the Super-hero — a blunt message which it required little skill to convey.

However, Nietzsche's victory was not achieved quite as easily as he had expected. Ariadne had resolved, as Nietzsche put it, that she would be the downfall, not only of the Theseus-figure Hans von Bülow, the first to succumb to her, but of all the heroes who came her way. Dionysus therefore shows her respect. 'Ariadne', he says, 'you are a labyrinth.' He too, behind whose mask crouched the figure of Wagner, would sooner or later meet his end in the maze and make way for the Super-hero. Eighteen years after the tragedy of the rejected Bülow — and five years after the death of Wagner — Nietzsche, similarly rejected, still saw the events of that time as though they had happened only the previous day. In a letter to Bülow, the cuckold of Tribschen, from Turin on 4 January 1889, only days before being taken to the mental asylum in Basel, he wrote: 'Having regard to the fact that you, a Hanseatic represen-tative, were the first, while I was only third in the line that leads to Madame Veuve Cliquot-Ariadne, I cannot spoil your game. Instead, I sentence you to *The Lion of Venice* [the opera by Köselitz] — I hope it devours you.'

Like his enigmatic missives to Cosima in the same period, this apparently absurd message alludes to the demands made by the new Dionysus on the bride abandoned by her hero. Bülow was Cosima's first lover: in calling him 'Hanseatic', Nietzsche puns on 'Hans Wurst', the clown of medieval German drama, a favourite word of Nietzsche's and an appropriate figure to represent Bülow. Her second lover, whose name he tactfully withholds, was Wagner, while the third is Nietzsche himself — or more precisely, the 'Dionysus' whose signature appears at the foot of the letter. The cipher he has thought up to denote Cosima combines a reference to her widowhood — recalling Ariadne's desolation — with the name of a famous champagne and the intoxicated Dionysus; as the favourite tipple of her late husband, Veuve Cliquot now promises the 'merry widow' an exhilarating future by the side of her third suitor. Given this development, the first Hans Wurst could do nothing but await his fate, namely to be devoured — not by the Minotaur, who has long since perished, but by the 'Venetian lion' of Köselitz's opera, which would soon strike fear into the hearts of Bayreuth audiences.

But first the widow had to be won over. In order to gain her sympathy, Nietzsche forgot all the criticisms he had heaped on her for turning the Master into an idol and began to woo her with extravagant praise, hailing her as 'the only woman I have ever revered' and 'by far the noblest person in the world'. He therefore felt justified — a Dionysus can do such things — in elevating her to the ranks of the gods, as he had done with his friend Erwin Rohde. Never, he went on, had he recognized the validity of her marriage to Wagner, on grounds of propriety. 'I always saw her union with Wagner as adultery pure and simple — the Tristan situation,' he wrote in a fragment for *Ecce Homo*. Bülow too had compared the scandal to 'the case of Tristan', a situation of which Nietzsche's sense of virtue could not but cause him to disapprove. At the same, time we catch glimpses of Dionysus' conviction that

14 Cosima Wagner, who survived not only her husband but also Nietzsche, her first husband Hans von Bülow and her son-in-law Houston Stewart Chamberlain.

he had been promised the hand of Princess Ariadne since before the time of Theseus, leaving her liaisons with the two earlier heroes as episodes of deceit and betrayal. Compared with the divine supremacy of her true lover, the crude, uncouth Wagner was like a buffoon, a 'Hans Wurst'. His encounter with Cosima-Ariadne, on the other hand, he described as 'the only time I found my equal'. Cosima, however, had no desire to see it this way.

The poem 'Ariadne's Lament' represented another attempt by Nietzsche to bring himself within the orbit of the goddess. The

Princess's tormented cry to the god to pierce her with his 'cruel barb' had originally been uttered by the character of the sorcerer in *Also sprach Zarathustra*, behind whom stood the figure of Wagner. Now it is from the mouth of the desperate Cosima that the erotic appeal is made to come: 'Return, O my unknown god, my pain, my highest joy!' The god, who had pursued her 'like a cruel huntsman' and inflicted pain upon her 'with his merciless weapon', hears her prayer at last and reveals himself as a mocking purveyor of riddles. Ridiculing her vanity by teasing her about her big ears, he uncovers a corner of the world of paradoxes in which he lives: 'Must we not hate each other before loving each other?' He leaves her with a final riddle to solve: 'I AM THY LABYRINTH.'

In one fell swoop the jesting philosopher had cast off his persona as the divine executioner. If one also strips him of the emerald apparel of the god Dionysus, nothing remains but a sick, diseased figure slowly succumbing to madness. First he had taken his cruel revenge on Wagner as the 'lascivious apostle of chastity'; then he savaged Cosima, swearing to show no mercy towards her interventions 'in matters of German culture, let alone of religion'. Finally, embarrassed and unsure of himself, he makes her his mysteriously coded declaration of love. Such has been the modern interpretation of his apostrophes to 'Princess Ariadne, my beloved'. But this was not how they were intended. 'I am thy labyrinth' conceals not a declaration of love but an entreaty to Cosima to reflect on this new truth, to reflect on *him.*

By approaching her in the guise of Dionysus, Nietzsche not only strengthened his claim on Cosima as Wagner's heir but also revealed his hitherto hidden nature as the god who is at the same time his own antithesis, the god who embodies at once the ecstasy of living and the torment of dying, joy and pain, a figure who is both man and woman. Cosima was aware of the rumours Wagner had spread about his disciple, rumours 'about that which we women can never understand'. Now that Nietzsche stood unveiled

as the deity of bisexuality, there was no longer any reason for him
to conceal the fact.

Back in Tribschen, at a time that from a distance appeared like
the prelude to a period of ideal harmony, he had opened the eyes
of his 'friend Cosima' to the world of the Greeks, about which she
had hitherto known little, a heroic, masculine world dominated by
the radiant figure of Apollo. Thanks to his interpretation of
antiquity, she told him, she had been able to find her way 'through
a labyrinth that would otherwise have surely remained
impenetrable'. Nietzsche forgot nothing. Now, eighteen years later,
he picked up her words and gave them a new Dionysian authority
– 'I am thy labyrinth', the world of antiquity, of homosexual love,
of the exultant Will to Power. This was to be the world, in contrast
to the claustrophobic, sensual, effeminate realm ruled over by
Wagner, to which she would in future be beholden. At the same
time Nietzsche conceded that she represented for him the same
fascinating antithesis that held him too, her mythological lover, in
its relentless grip. 'O Ariadne!' cries Dionysus. 'You are yourself
the labyrinth! There is no escape from you!' To which she replies:
'You flatter me, Dionysus, for you are a divine Being.' It is a reply
that suggests that she had grasped the situation a long while ago.
Embodying the labyrinth of his own femininity, she has at the
same time, without knowing what was happening to her, lost her
way in his labyrinth, that sinister part of her own self where the
god assaults her with his 'cruel barb' until, longing for him to
penetrate her, she finally yields to him.

Only with the 'wedding of Dionysus and Ariadne' do the rival
forces of masculine and feminine, enemies to the death, achieve
reconciliation. This was the real background to Nietzsche's
courtship of Wagner's widow, as he confided to Jacob Burckhardt
on 4 January 1889, at a time when he was already undergoing
psychiatric treatment in Turin. Twenty years earlier Burckhardt
had witnessed Nietzsche's obsession with the Wagners at

Tribschen. Now he received a message that read: 'My only role is, together with Ariadne, to represent the ideal balance of all forces.' The message was signed 'Dionysus'.

All his enticements and dithyrambs, all his teasing and wooing met with total silence. His vision of a divine union that would reconcile the differences between warring extremes accompanied him into the labyrinthine depths of the institutions in which he spent the last twelve years of his life. One may wonder whether, by consistently ignoring him, the iron lady of Bayreuth contributed to his tragic fate. Nietzsche himself must have believed it to be so. According to the records of the Jena mental asylum for 27 March 1889, he declared: 'It was my wife Cosima Wagner who brought me here.'

Bibliographical Note

General

For Cosima's letters to Nietzsche see *Die Briefe Cosima Wagners an Friedrich Nietzsche* (2 vols, Weimar, 1938–40). Cosima subsequently burnt a large proportion of Nietzsche's letters to her. His complete surviving correspondence is to be found in Giorgio Colli and Mazzino Montinari (eds), *Nietzsche: Briefwechsel: Kritische Gesamtausgabe* (Berlin/New York, 1975ff.). His surviving letters to Wagner and Cosima have also been published in the *Kritische Studienausgabe der Briefe Friedrich Nietzsches* (Munich, 1980; abbr. *KSB*). See also E. Thierbach (ed.) *Die Briefe Cosima Wagners an Friedrich Nietzsche* (Gesellschaft der Freunde des Nietzsche-Archivs, Nendeln/Liechtenstein, 1975).

Cosima's diaries (*Die Tagebucher Cosima Wagners* ed. M. Gregor-Dellin and D. Mack, Munich, 1976; translated by Geoffrey Skelton, London, 1978–80) give a day-by-day account of life in the Wagner household and the development of the Bayreuth cult from 1869 – the year Nietzsche first visited Wagner – to the composer's death in 1883. Her growing hostility towards Nietzsche from 1876 onwards is documented in her voluminous correspondence with her daughter Daniela (Stuttgart, 1933), with Houston Stewart Chamberlain (Leipzig, 1934), Prince Ernst zu Hohenlohe-Langenburg (Stuttgart, 1937), Ludwig Schemann (Regensburg, 1937), Richard Strauss (Tutzing, 1978) and others. A selection of letters from these and other relevant sources is to be found in D. Mack (ed.) *Cosima Wagner. Das zweite Leben*, (Munich, 1980).

Nietzsche's observations on Wagner and Cosima are to be found in the *Kritische Gesamtausgabe* of his works, edited by Colli and Montinari (Berlin, 1967ff). Individual references can be traced from the index of the *Kritische Studienausgabe* of Nietzsche's works (Munich, 1980; abbr. *KSA*). Wagner's comments on Nietzsche are recorded by Cosima in her diaries; many are also to be found in Wagner's so-called Brown Book edited by J. Bergfeld (Zurich/Freiburg, 1975; English translation by G. Bird, London, 1980). The standard work on the anti-Semitism of Bayreuth is H. Zelinsky, *Richard Wagner – ein deutsches Thema* (Berlin/Vienna, 1983).

As to the secondary literature, the various biographies of Wagner and Nietzsche contain little on the specific subject of the relationship between Nietzsche and Cosima. Works on Nietzsche, such as the fact-laden study by Curt Paul Janz (3 vols, Munich, 1978ff) and Werner Ross's *Der ängstliche Adler* (Munich, 1980), which turns him into a character from a tragi-comic novel, tend to present him as a genius the equal of Wagner, a man who shared with the great composer a moment of epoch-making significance in the history of the nineteenth century. Nietzsche as the apprentice manipulated by the Master for his own ends is a topic totally ignored. Among other general works are R.J. Hollingdale, *Nietzsche: The Man and his Philosophy* (London/Baton Rouge, 1965) and *Nietzsche* (London, 1973); F. Copleston, *Friedrich Nietzsche: Philosopher of Culture* (London/New York, 1975); and J.P. Stern, *A Study of Nietzsche* (Cambridge, 1979).

But wide of the mark as the description of the association between the two men as 'the friendship of the century' may be, no less misleading are those works that see Nietzsche as one who had it in him to become the leading apostle of the Wagnerian ideal but who for the basest of reasons betrayed the lord of Bayreuth and his lady (see, for example, M. Eger, Director of the Wagner Museum in Bayreuth, in his anti-Nietzsche book *Wenn ich Wagnern den Krieg mache . . .* , [Vienna, 1991]). Such works ascribe Nietzsche's behaviour to jealousy on account of Cosima, envy provoked by Wagner's rejection of him as a composer or simply megalomania. In his widely read biography of Wagner, *Richard Wagner. Sein Leben, sein Werk, sein Jahrhundert* (Munich 1980; trans. J.M. Brownjohn, London, 1983), Martin Gregor-Dellin passes over the political background and concentrates on the colourful aspects of a tragic love-hate relationship, while English biographies such as Ernest Newman, *The Life of Wagner* (4 vols, London 1933–46), R.W. Gutman, *Richard Wagner: The Man, his Mind and his Music* (London/New York, 1968) and R. Taylor, *Richard Wagner: His Life, Art and Thought* (London/New York, 1979) deal with the Nietzsche–Cosima relationship as part of the biographical narrative. The basic features of the relationship are delineated in J. Köhler,   *Zarathustras Geheimnis. Friedrich Nietzsche und seine verschlüsselte Botschaft* (Nördlingen, 1989; paperback edition Reinbek, 1992). The connection between Wagner and Hitler's Third Reich is analysed in J. Köhler, *Wagners Hitler. Der Prophet und sein Vollstrecker* (Munich, 1997).

To Individual Chapters

1 A Visit to the Underworld • On 'Ariadne's Lament' see W. Groddeck, Friedrich Nietzsches *Dionysos-Dithyramben* (Berlin, 1991). The dithyrambs have been translated into English by R.J. Hollingdale (London, 1984). – Details on Cosima Wagner's last years are to be found in Friedelind Wagner, *Nacht über Bayreuth* (Bern, 1945) and in H.J. Syberberg's television interview with Winifred Wagner in 1975. – On Nietzsche's final years see P.D. Volz, *Nietzsche im Labyrinth seiner Krankheit* (Würzburg, 1990), which confirms the long-held supposition that he was suffering from syphilis. S.L. Gilman (ed.), *Begegnungen mit Nietzsche* (Bonn, 1981) contains an extensive collection of reports by contemporaries on their encounters with Nietzsche.

2 Learning the Art of Self-Sacrifice • On Nietzsche's traumatic childhood experiences see J. Köhler, *op. cit.* and J. Kjaer, *Nietzsche. Die Zerstörung der Humanität durch 'Mutterliebe'* (Opladen, 1990). The most detailed account of Nietzsche's childhood and adolescence is given in J.J. Schmidt, *Nietzsche absconditus* (4 vols, Berlin, 1991ff), where the role played by Ernst Ortlepp, Nietzsche's early mentor, is described for the first time. – Among sources of information on Cosima's childhood see Richard Graf DuMoulin Eckart, *Cosima Wagner* (2 vols, trans. C.A. Phillips, New York, 1931) – a tendentious hagiography but rich in detail – and the more critical study by G.R. Marek, *Cosima Wagner: Ein Leben für ein Genie* (Bayreuth, 1982). A detailed and balanced portrait of Cosima is given by A. Walker in his three-volume biography of Liszt (London, 1983ff); see also the biographies of Liszt by Sacheverell Sitwell (London, 1955) and R. Taylor (London, 1986). The dramatic scene when Hans von Bülow discovered his wife's adultery with Wagner is described in H. Conrad, 'Der Beidler-Konflikt', *Bayreuther Festspielnachrichten*, 1982

3 The Euphoric Acolyte and 4 Lessons in Subjugation • The principal sources are Nietzsche's letters and Cosima's diaries. Wagner's *Parzival* sketch of 1865 is in his Brown Book.

5 'Will Dionysus Flee from Ariadne?' • Nietzsche's scattered notes on *Empedokles* are collected by J. Söring, 'Nietzsches Empedokles-Plan', *Nietzsche-Studien* 19, Berlin/New York, 1990. – On Nietzsche's 'satyr drama' see *KSA* 12, 401ff.

6 The Spirit that Begets Tragedy • Nietzsche's fragment written in the first weeks of 1871 (*KSA* 7, 333ff) was later revised as 'Der griechische Staat' (*KSA* 1, 764ff), one of 'Five Prefaces to Five Unwritten Books'. – The quotations from Wagner are from 'Die Kunst und die Revolution' (W. Golther [ed.], *Gesammelte Schriften und Dichtungen*, [Berlin, 1914],

III, 10ff) and 'Das Kunstwerk der Zukunft' (ed. cit. III, 134ff). Nietzsche's sketches for his essay on David Friedrich Strauss, the first of his four *Unzeitgemässe Betrachtungen*, are in *KSA* 7, 584ff.

7 Bayreuth Perspectives • Peter Cornelius's remarks on Wagner are in his *Ausgewählte Briefe*, ed. Carl Maria Cornelius (Leipzig, 1904–5) and in Carl Maria Cornelius, *Peter Cornelius, Der Wort- und Tondichter* (Regensburg, 1925). – Wagner's reference to Nietzsche and Rohde as 'Greek youths' comes in his Brown Book, 232. – On Rohde's letters to his fiancée see A. Patzer, 'Erwin Rohde in Bayreuth', *Nietzsche-Studien* 20, Berlin/NewYork, 1991.

8 'Cherchez le Juif' • On Nietzsche's last meeting with Wagner and Cosima see Malwida von Meysenbug, *Der Lebensabend einer Idealistin* (2 vols, Berlin, 1917, II, 235ff) and *Memoiren einer Idealistin* (Stuttgart/Berlin/Leipzig, 1927), as well as Elisabeth Förster-Nietzsche, *Wagner und Nietzsche zur Zeit ihrer Freundschaft* (Munich, 1915, 265ff). For Cosima's letters to Marie von Wolkenstein see DuMoulin Eckart, op. cit., II, 842ff. – Nietzsche's notes on his last conversation with Wagner are in *KSA* 14, 161ff. – Concerning Wagner's attacks on Nietzsche and the Jews see *KSA* 15, 84ff.

9 A Mortal Insult • On the correspondence between Wagner and Dr Eiser see C. von Westernhagen, *Richard Wagner* (Zurich, 1956, 524ff) and L. Lütkehaus, *'O Wollust, O Hölle'* (Frankfurt, 1992, 201ff). Allusion to the subject of sodomy was already made by Josef Hofmiller in 'Nietzsche', *Süddeutsche Monatshefte* 2, November 1931, 89. – Cosima's blackmail letter of December 1865 to King Ludwig II of Bavaria is among her unpublished correspondence transcribed in Bayreuth by Martha Schad. – Dr Eiser's account of Nietzsche's fit of rage is in Gilman, op. cit. 345. – On Nietzsche's visions of suicide see *KSA* 8, 504ff.

10 Return to the Underworld • The majority of Cosima's outbursts against Nietzsche are included in *Cosima Wagner. Das zweite Leben*, ed. cit. Her observations on *Also sprach Zarathustra* occur in her correspondence with Houston Stewart Chamberlain (ed. cit., 608ff). On Hitler's plans for a Nietzsche memorial see D.F. Hoffmann, *Zur Geschichte des Nietzsche-Archivs* (Berlin, 1991, 111ff) and 'Hitlers Wagner-Akropolis für Bayreuth', in F. Spotts, *Bayreuth* (New Haven, 1994, 196ff). – Nietzsche's 'Madame Veuve Cliquot-Ariadne' letter is in *KSB* 8, 573. – On Nietzsche's last enigmatic words, 'My wife Cosima Wagner brought me here', see Volz, op. cit., 397.

Index

Plato influenced by 90; RW covets
'Jewish artefact' 61–2; *see also* anti-
Semitism

Keller, Gottfried 98
Kögel, Fritz 144
Köselitz, Heinrich (Peter Gast) 55,
132–3, 133–4, 142–3, 144, 156; *The
Lion of Venice* 169–70, 171, 172

labyrinth *see* Dionysus: and Ariadne myth
Lassalle, Ferdinand 49
Laube, Heinrich 17, 18
Leipzig, Germany 17–18, 20, 58
Lenbach, Franz von 8, 80
Levi, Hermann 128–9, 139
Liszt, Anna (grandmother of CW) 22, 87
Liszt, Blandine-Rachel (sister of CW) 8, 22, 24, 25–6, 87
Liszt, Daniel (brother of CW) 8, 22, 25, 87
Liszt, Franz (father of CW) 8, 27, 28, *29*, 30, 56, 123, 150; anti-Semitism 87; approves of von Bülow 26; as father 22, 23, 24, 25; friendship with Wagners 113; *Legend of St Elisabeth* 46, 50; love affairs 23; opposes CW's divorce 34–5; RW's affection for 105
Ludwig II, King of Bavaria 171; CW detects similarities with N 107, 154; CW manipulates 34, 101–2, 153–4; homosexual tendencies 152–4; letter to RW 20, 21; in love with RW 34, 105; *Parsifal* written for 50, 51; as patron to RW 8, 34, 35, 41, 47, 123; Wagners urge to marry 103
Luther, Martin 106

Maier, Mathilde 29, 31
Makart, Hans 75
Mannheim Music Festival 57
Marek, George 150
Marie (dancer and RW's mistress) 31
masturbation: RW perceives evils of 147, 150
Maura, Seraphine 100, 101
Mayer, Hans 119
Mendelssohn, Felix 38, 41, 94
Meyer & Noske (jewellers) 62
Meyer, Friederike 31
Meysenbug, Malwida von 159; at Mannheim music festival 57; CW corresponds with 104, 107, 131, 154; N attacks RW to 162, 169; N tells of

'mortal insult' 140, 141, 143, 144; N's hostess in Sorrento 125, 126, 127, 129–31, 156; RW recommends baptism to 128
Minotaur *see* Dionysus: and Ariadne myth
Montinari, Mazzino 119
Mrazek, Anna 32
Münchener Neueste Nachrichten 153
Mussolini, Benito 168

Naumberg, Germany 15–16
Neue Zeitschrift für Musik 93
Newman, Ernest 87, 93
Nietzsche, Carl Ludwig (father of N) 15, 17
Nietzsche, Elisabeth *see* Förster-Nietzsche, Elisabeth
Nietzsche, Franziska (mother of N) 10, 15–16, 117, 143
Nietzsche, Friedrich Wilhelm *11*, *19*, *59*, *109*; aesthetic brotherhood idea 116; anti-Christianity 91, 92, 140–41; anti-Semitism 39, 79–80, 87–97, 162; Bülow receives absurd missive from 171–2; cruelty and sexuality 170; described as skittish 100–101; destruction fantasies 71, 92; Dionysus and Ariadne myth 1–7, 33, 36, 53–4, 67, 72–4, 136–8, 170–76; on female role 74; German mythology revived in *Geburt* 91–2;
HEALTH: diarrhoea 114; eye trouble 113, 144, 154, 159; haemorrhoids 78; hallucinatory experiences 55–6, 58; headaches 16, 58, 110, 113, 144, 159; hydrotherapy to be avoided 145, 147; hypochondria 99; insomnia 58, 78; madness 3–4, 6–7, 10–13, 36, 71, 163, 171–2, 175–6; nervous problems 70, 78, 163; nightmares 15, 16, 23, 54; overworked in Basel 58–9; suicidal thoughts 139–40, 156; syphilis 7, 159; war impairs 70
LIFE AND CAREER: in Bayreuth 98–117; childhood and school 15–18, 55; cult following 158, 159, 165–9; death 14; Hitler proposes memorial to 168-9; as medical orderly in Franco-Prussian war 68, 70, 77; professorship at Basel 37–8, 44, 58, 64, 78, 117; student in Leipzig 17–18, 58; success accompanied by madness 10–13; visit from Hitler 13
MUSICAL ABILITY: appreciation 11–12,